Pray More

Donna K. Maltese

STRESS LESS

Pray More

A Woman's
Devotional Guide to
Tranquil Living

BARBOUR BOOKS
An Imprint of Barbour Publishing, Inc.

Our mission is to inspire the world with the life-changing message of the Bible.

Member of the
Evangelical Christian
Publishers Association

Printed in the United States of America.

Introduction

More prevalent in the world today than ever before, stress affects twice as many women as men. We're anxious about everything from piles of laundry and doctors' bills to job security and the economy. Amid all these worries, we are surrounded by the noise of technology and information overload. But God has a time-tested solution: prayer.

To help women navigate their way through stress and into the peace of God's presence, we introduce this devotional guide featuring 180 readings and prayers based on this promise: "Make sure that you don't get so absorbed and exhausted in taking care of all your day-by-day obligations that you lose track of the time and doze off, oblivious to God. . . . Be up and awake to what God is doing! God is putting the finishing touches on the salvation work he began when we first believed" (Romans 13:11–12 MSG).

Each reading is designed to teach a woman how to live in God's freedom and reinforces the truth that with her focus on Him, she can reconnect with the power and peace to live a more wonder-filled life every day.

Read on to stress less and pray more!

Our Avenue

"Let not your hearts be troubled. Believe in God;
believe also in me. . . . Peace I leave with you; my peace
I give to you. Not as the world gives do I give to you.
Let not your hearts be troubled, neither let them be afraid."
JOHN 14:1, 27 ESV

Stress is nothing to be ashamed of. It's just a signal to be recognized and addressed. The problem is when we let stress take over, try to ignore it, or imagine we can handle it in our own strength.

God knew we'd have trouble in this life, that we'd find ourselves with anxiety-causing stress. But He also gave us a way out: Jesus. Our faith in Him is our avenue to an out-of-this-world peace.

Jesus is waiting. Take a deep belly breath. Exhale. Enter that secret place where He abides. Ask Him to cover you with His wings, to raise you up. To give you the word you need to hear, the peace you need to inhale.

I'm here, Lord, limp in Your arms.
Please fill me with Your peace.

Attuned to God

*"Give in to God, come to terms with him and
everything will turn out just fine. Let him
tell you what to do; take his words to heart."*
JOB 22:21–22 MSG

How many times do we not let God in on our plans, run ahead of what He has planned, and miss the blessings He's waiting to pour out on us?

Perhaps it's time to stop trying to figure things out on our own, thinking we know best. Maybe our thoughts and feet should come to a screeching halt. This just might be the day we get it right.

Consider spending some time in the Word and in prayer, allowing God to lead the way. Know that with God on your side, everything is and will be fine. Open up your mind to the wisdom and insight He has for you. Store His words in your heart. Then, and only then, attuned to and in step with Him, walk on.

*Lord, I'm so tired of trying to do all this on my own.
Show me what You would have me do, be, and see.*

Above the Storms

*Peter got out of the boat and walked on the water and
came to Jesus. But when he saw the wind, he was afraid,
and beginning to sink he cried out, "Lord, save me." Jesus
immediately reached out his hand and took hold of him.*
MATTHEW 14:29–31 ESV

At times, stress is like a storm raging within and without,
drawing our attention away from God bit by bit. Then, when
we suddenly realize our eyes are no longer on Him and our
ears are deaf to His voice, we begin to sink. That's because we're
looking at the waves instead of Jesus. We're listening to the
howling wind instead of the Holy Whisperer. Before we know it,
fear has supplanted our faith and we're in danger of drowning.

The remedy? Make Jesus your main attraction. Fix your eyes
on the Water Walker. Keep your ears open to His Word. In so
doing, you'll be riding above the storms within and without.

*Jesus, help me to keep You in the forefront of my
heart and mind, for You alone are my safe haven.*

Watch Where You're Going

Let your eyes look right on [with fixed purpose],
and let your gaze be straight before you.
PROVERBS 4:25 AMPC

One way a woman gets stressed out is by not living in the moment. She's wondering about all the what-ifs. She's consumed by all the what'll-happens of tomorrow. And all the could'ves, would'ves, and should'ves of yesterday. But worrying about the future and ruminating about the past only serve to ruin her present. Not only that, but such distractions from the now also set her up for a major fall because her eyes have left the path laid out for her.

The safer route is for her to leave all those stressors by the wayside. To focus on taking one step at a time, knowing that God intends for all things to work out for her good—no worries. To simply walk on the faith side—and let all else be.

Lord, give me the wisdom to watch my way,
knowing You have already gone before me and
made the path safe for my feet—and heart.

Strength for the Journey

"Arise and eat, for the journey is too great for you."
1 KINGS 19:7 ESV

Even God's most faithful can find themselves stressed out. Consider Elijah. After his victory with God, Elijah received a threatening message from Jezebel. Yet instead of waiting for a word from God, this prophet ran for his life. Over eighty miles later, Elijah sat down under a broom tree, asked God to take his life, and fell asleep.

God responded by sending Elijah an angel who touched him, said, "Arise and eat," and provided him with bread and water, giving Elijah enough strength for his next steps.

When you feel threatened, remember God and what He has done for you time and again. Tap into the knowledge that nothing can withstand His power. Wait for His word. But if you find yourself already on the run, remember that He will provide for you no matter where you go. Just rest in Him—He'll give you hope and strength for the next steps.

Thank You, Lord, for providing for me no matter where I go.

His Story

What are you doing here?
1 KINGS 19:9 AMPC

On Horeb, the mount of God, Elijah reaches a cave and sets up camp. There God asks—not once, but twice—"What are you doing here?" In response, Elijah tells God—not once, but twice—his story. How he's been fighting for God. But the Israelites don't seem to care. Other prophets have been murdered and the people are now looking to kill him, the only one of God's prophets left!

Yet God knows the true story, His story. He knows more prophets are left (see 1 Kings 18:4). That Jezebel is the only one who has threatened him. That Elijah seems to have forgotten His previous mighty acts.

When we replace God's story with our own, nothing but despair echoes in our heads. That's because our feelings have usurped God's truth. The story in our mind has overtaken His story for our lives. That's when we know it's time to change the thoughts in our head and get back to the true story.

Lord, help me to zero in on Your story for my life.

A Heart for Hearing

A quiet voice asked, "So Elijah,
now tell me, what are you doing here?"
1 KINGS 19:13 MSG

Not happy with Elijah's initial version of events, God tells him to come out of his cave and stand on the mountain. A strong wind comes by, breaking up the rocks. But God isn't in the wind. Then an earthquake—but still no God. Then a fire—but still no God. After the fire, in the silence that remains, comes a gentle voice. A whisper. That's when Elijah comes out of the cave, still hiding from God, masking his face with his cloak. As Elijah stands there, God asks him again, "What are you doing here?" And Elijah repeats his tale of woe and desperation.

God asks you to have a heart for His message. To stand before Him with boldness. To calmly listen. When you do, you will hear His still, small voice in the silence of your days.

Lord, help me to have a heart for Your message as I boldly
come before You, calmly listening for Your whisper.

Going Back

"Go back the way you came through the desert."
1 Kings 19:15 MSG

God directs Elijah to go back the way he'd come, which would put less and less distance between himself and the threats of Jezebel, the evil queen (and wife of King Ahab of Israel) he'd just run away from. Then, once he got there, Elijah's orders were, among other things, to anoint Jehu to be the new king over Israel!

Sooner or later, we will face circumstances in which we feel threatened. When we give in to our flesh, we may run away in fear and despair, only to find later that, having rediscovered God and heard His instructions, we have to go back and deal with the situation. That's when we must focus on the fact that God has the upper hand in any situation we find ourselves facing, that He will provide for us while we are back in the desert, and that He will help us find the courage to confront what frightened us in the first place.

I'm focused on Your power, Lord.
Help me to face whatever lies ahead.

Jesus on Board

*Then they were quite willing and glad for Him
to come into the boat. And now the boat went
at once to the land they had steered toward.*
JOHN 6:21 AMPC

Jesus having gone off to a mountain to pray, His disciples decided to head home across the sea. So they got into a boat and started rowing. As the darkness increased, Jesus was still a no-show. Meanwhile, the going got tough as a violent wind whipped up the waves. After straining against the oars for three or four miles, the disciples suddenly saw someone walking on the water near them. Their imaginations went wild and they became terrified. Jesus then calmed their fears, saying, "It is I; be not afraid!" (verse 20 AMPC).

When you're straining at the oars, be courageous and keep your eyes open for Jesus. When you see Him, invite Him to come aboard. Before you know it, you'll find yourself attaining that for which you were striving.

*Oh mighty Navigator of my life,
bring me toward the shore for which I strive!*

Keep Calm

*"When reports come in of wars and rumored wars,
keep your head and don't panic. This is
routine history; this is no sign of the end."*
MATTHEW 24:6 MSG

These days, just listening to the news can be a major stressor. For you hear of wars not only between nations but within nations. Then there are the wars on drugs, sex trafficking, opioid addiction, and so on. It's enough to discourage and dishearten even the most stoic of listeners.

Yet Jesus tells you not to panic. To keep your head. That this is just how it is. Meanwhile, what are you to do to keep calm and carry on?

One solution is to limit your exposure to the news. Find a level you can tolerate and maintain it. Another is to pray for all those involved in wars. Above all, replace those world worries with God's wisdom. Pray and memorize Bible verses to help you stay above the fray. Here's one to start you off:

*"You will keep in perfect peace all who trust in you,
all whose thoughts are fixed on you!"* [Isaiah 26:3 NLT].

Trust and Pray

*Trust God from the bottom of your heart; don't try
to figure out everything on your own. Listen for
God's voice in everything you do, everywhere you go;
he's the one who will keep you on track.*

PROVERBS 3:5–6 MSG

One surefire way to keep a lot of stress out of your life is to trust God. Do so from the very core of your being—mentally, physically, emotionally, and spiritually. Believe His promises, that He means all things for your good. That He loves you more than any other person you know. That He has a plan for your life. That He has got not only your back but also your front.

Don't depend on yourself and your own finite ideas. Instead, depend on the One who is part of infinity itself, who sees a way beyond current appearances and impressions. Who knows your future—and your past.

Pray. Tell God what's happening. Ask Him to speak. Then actually listen to what He says. Do what He tells you to do. Pray more, stress less.

Lord, here I am. Tell me what to do.

Seeking Approval

I'm not trying to win the approval of people,
but of God. If pleasing people were my goal,
I would not be Christ's servant.
GALATIANS 1:10 NLT

Abraham Lincoln said, "You can please some of the people all of the time, you can please all of the people some of the time, but you can't please all of the people all of the time." Yet that is exactly what we sometimes try to do. And in the process, we end up getting stressed out, because pleasing everyone is an unattainable goal. We are looking for love and approval in all the wrong places. But what's a girl to do?

Look for God's approval only. Don't worry what other people might say or do. It's Him you're looking to please. It's in Him you feel secure. It's He who loves you beyond measure, who has created you for a specific reason. So make Him number one in your life, seeking to live for Him alone.

I hope to please You, Lord, in all I say,
think, and do. Show me how to serve You!

Follow Him

And rising very early in the morning,
while it was still dark, he departed and went
out to a desolate place, and there he prayed.
MARK 1:35 ESV

Jesus was up against a lot of different political and religious factions. He was pressed by the crowds that were seeking healing physically, emotionally, mentally, and spiritually. He was teaching and training disciples who just didn't seem to get it right. He was pressured by Satan who was trying to tempt Him away from His mission. He encountered people in His own hometown—even family members—who either didn't believe Him or wanted Him to tip His hand before it was time.

Yet in spite of all the things He was up against, Jesus never panicked but kept His peace. How? He went off alone and sought His Father God. He left the crowds and went to a deserted and desolate place. Somewhere secluded where He could meet with God one-on-one in the quiet of the morning hours.

Follow Him.

Lord, I come to You now, alone, seeking Your face.

Choices

Then Jehoshaphat said to the king of Israel,
"But first, find out what the Lord's word is in this matter."
1 Kings 22:5 gw

King Ahab wanted to try to reclaim some territory. But Jehoshaphat, king of Judah, wasn't taking one step until he asked the Lord's advice.

When we make choices without first consulting the Lord—or even worse, when we do things against His advice—we can end up not only feeling stressed out but also facing ruin. So for less stress in your life, be like the wise Jehoshaphat. Seek God's advice before you choose. Pray, "Make your ways known to me, O Lord, and teach me your paths. Lead me in your truth and teach me because you are God, my savior. I wait all day long for you" (Psalm 25:4–5 gw).

Know that God will give you all the wisdom you need for where you are and will keep you from tripping up on your path (see Psalm 25:14–15).

Give me light for my path, Lord.
I'm not moving until You speak.

The Upside

When troubles of any kind come your way,
consider it an opportunity for great joy.
JAMES 1:2 NLT

We all sometimes find ourselves going through dark days, groping for a way out. But there is an upside to these times: when we are tested, we come out better and stronger than before.

Consider the Old Testament hero Joseph who was thrown into a pit, sold to traders, and imprisoned unjustly. Yet he went on to become the number two man in Egypt. Why? Because no matter what happened to him, no matter where he landed, he had faith that "the Lord was with him and made whatever he did to prosper" (Genesis 39:23 AMPC; see also 39:2)!

Even though you might not be where you'd like to be, don't stress about it. Just have faith. Know that God is with you. He's building up your resilience, bringing out the best in you, training you up for the next steps as He prospers you right where you are.

Lord, help me to find joy wherever I land, knowing You're
there, helping me not just to survive but to thrive!

Look Up

*I press on to reach the end of the race and receive the heavenly
prize for which God, through Christ Jesus, is calling us.*
PHILIPPIANS 3:14 NLT

God has given us a vision for our lives. We are reaching for the
prize that is awaiting us, that to which Jesus is calling us. We
have something to strive for.

Thus we need not get caught up in the cycle of bad news.
We need not lose hope. We can choose to see God before us,
feel Jesus' warm breath upon us, hear the Spirit's voice within
us, giving us guidance, telling us to keep our cool.

Have your eyes been glued to the ground? Are you dragging
your feet? Is your chin on your chest? Look up to what God is
doing. Keep your eyes on His heavenly prize. Know that God
has a purpose for your life and that He will brighten up whatever
darkness may come your way.

*My eyes are on You, Jesus. I'm walking in Your light,
feeling Your breath, hearing Your voice.*

Not Knowing

*We have no might to stand against this great
company that is coming against us. We do not
know what to do, but our eyes are upon You.*
2 CHRONICLES 20:12 AMPC

God is thrilled when we are humble, when we admit we have
no idea what to do but are looking to Him for help, wisdom,
guidance, and direction. At the same time, admitting to ourselves
that we don't know what to do takes all the pressure off us! In
fact, much of our strength lies in believing God. What a relief
that we don't need to have all the answers! How wonderful to
admit—even to our spouses, children, and friends, if we must—
that we don't know what to do next but are looking to God.

Know that God will always come through, no matter how
bad things may look. He'll take care of all that's coming against
you. He'll bring you out of whatever crisis you find yourself in.

*Thank You, God, that I don't need to have all
the answers—because You have them for me!*

Level Ground

Jesus said to those Jews who had believed in Him,
If you abide in My word [hold fast to My teachings and live
in accordance with them], you are truly My disciples. And
you will know the Truth, and the Truth will set you free.
JOHN 8:31–32 AMPC

The quaking of our worlds—inner and outer—can leave us shaken. But God provides us with solutions. He helps us to be resilient, to absorb the shocks that come our way, to hold fast under the pressure.

God's Word repeatedly tells us not to be afraid. He has blessed us with the avenue of prayer. He invites and encourages us to abide in Him, promising that when we walk in His truth, when we believe His Word with our whole heart, mind, body, and soul, we are freed from the sins that snare, the worries that stress. And in so doing, we find His love spread out before us and our feet standing on level ground (see Psalm 26:3, 12).

I find my freedom in You, Lord Jesus.

Enlightened Eyes of Faith

"It wasn't you who sent me here, but God."
GENESIS 45:8 GW

The Old Testament Joseph easily could have considered himself a victim of his circumstances and the people in his life. He could have blamed his brothers for throwing him in a pit and selling him to traders. He could have blamed Potiphar and his wife for his imprisonment. He could have blamed the baker and the wine bearer for leaving him to dream in the dark dungeon. But he never did. Instead, he persevered, believing that God, the Ruler of the universe, was with him, would protect him, and would turn his trials into triumphs. And so He did.

How would your outlook change if you realized that all things, people, and situations—both wonderful and awful—are part of God's plan for your life and that He will be with you through it all? Only through the enlightened eyes of your faith will you see God's caring hand in the world's darkness.

*Thank You, God, for working out Your good will
in all things and sticking with me through it all.*

Take a Breath

[It is] the Spirit of God that made me
[which has stirred me up], and the breath of the
Almighty that gives me life [which inspires me].
JOB 33:4 AMPC

What do you do when the flight, fight, or freeze button has been pushed and stress has taken over? When you can't seem to get your bearings and just need a way to calm down?

Pause. Become aware of what's going on mentally, physically, spiritually, and emotionally. Remind yourself that God is with you. Then, through several deep belly breaths, reconnect with the Source of all creation. Link up with the God who breathed life into you, as He did Adam (see Genesis 2:7). Find your way back to Jesus, who breathed the Word of life into His followers (see John 20:22). Recite God's words, "Be still, and know that I am God" (Psalm 46:10 NLT). Before you know it, you will feel yourself connected with the Holy Spirit (which, in Hebrew, is *ruakh*, meaning "wind" or "air in motion").

Lord, in this breath I come to You.
Please bring peace to my soul and spirit.

Powerful Pauses

The LORD is my light and my salvation.
Who is there to fear?
PSALM 27:1 GW

Mystery writer Arthur Somers Roche wrote, "Worry is a thin stream of fear trickling through the mind. If encouraged, it cuts a channel into which all other thoughts are drained." But God would have you look to Him, rely on Him, gain your strength, confidence, and courage from Him. The key is to pause when you feel a bit unsettled. Check in with your emotions. Accept them for what they are: merely a reflection of what you're thinking.

Then become aware of what you're thinking. If your inner dialogue is against what God would have you believe, replace it with His truth. Then choose to own and live that truth. Not just in that moment but in every moment, day after day after day. By forming the habit of replacing your inner talk with God's truth, you'll soon be on His wavelength, living the life He's planned for you.

I pause, Lord, to accept my feelings, align my
thoughts with Yours, and live in Your truth.

One Thing

"Martha, Martha, you are anxious and troubled about many things, but one thing is necessary. Mary has chosen the good portion, which will not be taken away from her."
LUKE 10:41–42 ESV

The more we worry, the less we pray. And the more we pray, the less we worry. So why not pray? But not just by saying the same old prayer over and over. Or reading the same old devotional. Or repeating the same old psalm. Instead, get some new ideas, words, books, verses. Why not actually imagine yourself at Jesus' feet, forgetting about all the to-dos you need to get done?

You gift a lot of people with your time, sometimes more than you have to spare! But how much of your time are you gifting to God? Take stock and stop. Sit. Listen with both ears. Choose that good part: being at your Master's feet. Gift Him with those precious moments, and He will gift you with peace of mind, body, heart, spirit, and soul.

Lord, here I am. At Your feet.
Leaning back into Your presence.

Practicing Truth

If we claim that we experience a shared life with him and continue to stumble around in the dark, we're obviously lying through our teeth—we're not living what we claim.
1 JOHN 1:6 MSG

Winston Churchill is credited with saying, "Men occasionally stumble over the truth, but most of them pick themselves up and hurry off as if nothing ever happened." Although at first this quote may sound silly, it has the ring of truth about it.

How many times has God pointed out a truth to you, one that would help smooth your walk in this life, yet afterward, after the initial aha moment, you walked on as usual, allowing life to woo you away as if you'd never stumbled upon the truth in the first place?

God wants us walking with Jesus. The more we walk in His truth, the more light there will be for the path before us and the less stress and trip-ups we'll encounter.

What truth is God asking you to practice?

Lord, show me the truth You want me to live and walk in.

Heart to Heart

You have said, Seek My face [inquire for and require My presence as your vital need]. My heart says to You, Your face (Your presence), Lord, will I seek, inquire for, and require [of necessity and on the authority of Your Word].
PSALM 27:8 AMPC

God wants you to seek His face, for He knows that when you do, your heart, mind, and spirit will have their true focus. You will find His peace, His strength, His way. You will be more in line with His will for you because you have looked to Him before you even set your foot out the door or stuck your toe in the water.

Your spirit needs God's presence just as your body needs air, food, and water. God is aching to hear your voice. He's ready for that heart-to-heart talk that will energize you for the day. Seek. Speak. Listen. Then walk.

Here I am, Lord, coming before You, seeking Your presence, breathing in Your Spirit, drinking in Your light, feeding on Your wisdom. Show me Your way.

Always There

The Lord is the Refuge and Stronghold of my life. . . . Though a host encamp against me, my heart shall not fear; though war arise against me, [even then] in this will I be confident.
PSALM 27:1, 3 AMPC

Every woman wants a place where she can run and hide when things get tough. A place to reset, refuel, regain her composure before she says or does something she knows she'll regret. Of course, the woman who walks in the Way knows that place is in God, who is her stronghold. She knows He is always there waiting to help, to strengthen, to shower her with love, peace, joy, and confidence, to empower her to do all He's calling her to do.

How does she get there? By taking a mental and emotional pause. Delving deep within to find His presence, light, warmth, and assurance. Spending however much time she needs in that place. And then, and only then, moving forward in His name.

*With You in my life, in my heart,
I fear nothing. You, Lord, are my all in all.*

Angels—No Strangers

*He will give His angels [especial] charge over you to accompany
and defend and preserve you in all your ways [of obedience
and service]. They shall bear you up on their hands.*
PSALM 91:11–12 AMPC

Women are no strangers to angels. An angel found Hagar fleeing
Sarah and told Hagar to go back and submit; she obeyed and
her son became a leader of many nations. Angels rescued Lot's
wife from God's wrath on Sodom but couldn't rescue her from
looking back; when she gave in to her longing for the past, she
became a pillar of salt. An angel appeared to Manoah's barren
wife, telling her to take care of herself because she would soon
be bearing a son. The angel Gabriel came to Mary, telling her that
she was not to fear, the Lord was with her, she'd soon bear a son,
and nothing was impossible with God! After Jesus' crucifixion,
an angel told His female followers not to be afraid. Jesus lives!

Rest easy and assured. God's angels are watching over you.

Thank You, Lord, for Your heavenly protection.

Counter Acts

"Oh, how my soul praises the Lord. How my spirit rejoices in God my Savior! For he took notice of his lowly servant girl. . . . For the Mighty One is holy, and he has done great things for me. . . . His mighty arm has done tremendous things!"
LUKE 1:46–49, 51 NLT

Studies have shown that keeping a gratitude journal reduces your stress! That's because people who count their blessings are more focused on how good things are. These "counter acts" naturally counteract stress, making blessing counters more resilient and more able to face whatever comes their way!

When was the last time you thanked God? What did you thank Him for? How can you make counting your blessings part of your regular routine?

Consider listing at least five things you're grateful for before going to bed at night. Doing so will not only make you a more optimistic, content, and joyful person, but it will help you sleep better!

Lord of my life, my heart rejoices in
You as my lips thank You for. . .

A Simple Thing

*"You will see neither wind nor rain. . .but this valley will be
filled with water. You will have plenty. . . . But this is only a
simple thing for the LORD, for he will make you victorious."*
2 KINGS 3:17–18 NLT

———

You're up against it, with no idea what to do. Nor any idea of
what God might do.

But here's the good news: God has a plan. One you cannot
even begin to imagine. The only thing you need to remember,
to rely on, is that what seems like an impossible task, an
insurmountable problem, an unbelievable situation is nothing
to God. For Him, it's "only a simple thing." He's going to make
you victorious. Your role? To remind yourself that God is in
control and to trust Him to whom the solution is a simple thing.

"The next day. . .water suddenly appeared! . . . Soon there
was water everywhere" (2 Kings 3:20 NLT).

*I know You're going to work it all out, Lord.
So here I am, leaving this "simple thing" in Your hands.*

Committed Seafarers

Commit your actions to the LORD,
and your plans will succeed.
PROVERBS 16:3 NLT

The Roman philosopher Lucius Annaeus Seneca said, "If a man does not know to what port he is steering, no wind is favorable to him." That's enough to make a woman stop and think about her plans.

When we're not focused on where we think God wants us to go, we feel as if we're getting nowhere. This lack of direction can lead to stress, the stress a seafarer may feel when all she seems to be doing is wandering around the oceans, trying not to get shipwrecked by a storm, and feeling lost with no safe port in sight.

You know God has a purpose for your life. Be assured that as long as you put everything you're doing in His hands—leaving the results to Him and Him alone—not only will your stress abate, but God will make your plans succeed.

Lord, I'm looking to You to help me navigate these waters.
I commit all my plans and works to You.

Hanging On Tight

*The minute I said, "I'm slipping, I'm falling," your love,
GOD, took hold and held me fast. When I was upset and
beside myself, you calmed me down and cheered me up.*
PSALM 94:18–19 MSG

Nothing this week, month, year, has worked out right. No matter
how hard you try, nothing seems to be going your way. You
are not only stressed out but also feeling helpless, as if you're
falling and no one is waiting to catch you.

Tell God how you're feeling, how much pressure you're
under, how alone and hopeless you feel. As soon as you do,
He'll grab hold of you and hang on tight. He'll calm you down,
open your eyes to the blessings around you, and put a smile
back on your face.

What are you waiting for? Take advantage of the One who
has chosen you and vowed to walk with you, to talk to you like
a friend. The One who will never, ever let you go.

*Jesus, I feel as if I'm slipping, falling.
Grab on to me. Never let me go.*

Just Because

"Don't be afraid; you are more valuable
to God than a whole flock of sparrows."
MATTHEW 10:31 NLT

In the Bible, God consistently tells His people to be still, take a break from the everyday stress and strain, step out of this crazy world, and get to know Him (see Psalm 46:10). But it sometimes seems that before we can do this, we have to come to terms with the fact that God loves and values us just the way we are. Pastor and author Max Lucado puts it this way: "You are valuable because you exist. Not because of what you do or what you have done, but simply because you are."

Let your stress melt away as you spend some time in God's presence today with the knowledge that there is nothing you must do to prove yourself to Him. You can have the greatest relationship with your Creator just by hanging with Him and knowing He loves you just because you're you.

Thank You, Lord, for loving me just the way I am.

Reap the Joys

*Let's see how inventive we can be in encouraging
love and helping out, not avoiding worshiping
together as some do but spurring each other on.*
HEBREWS 10:24–25 MSG

Stress can affect us in a variety of ways, including mentally, physically, and emotionally. One way to keep ourselves happy and healthy in all those areas is to connect with like-minded people, that is, other Christians. And what better way to do that than through church! Gather for worship with fellow believers. Find or found a ministry that feeds a passion in your own life. Perhaps a knitting and crocheting group that makes prayer shawls, a quilting group that makes blankets, a cooking group that helps at soup kitchens, a landscaping group that commits random acts of kindness in people's yards or along the highways.

Before you know it, you'll be distancing yourself from the fallow fields of stress and forging new ground where you can reap the joys of serving and encouraging others.

*Show me, Lord, what passion I can pursue that can,
at the same time, serve others—in Your love and name!*

A Godly Guffaw

A cheerful disposition is good for your health;
gloom and doom leave you bone-tired.
PROVERBS 17:22 MSG

So many sources of news are vying for our attention. The anchorperson tells us war is in our midst or just over the horizon. The radio broadcasts the latest shooting. The meteorologist warns us of the next hurricane, drought, earthquake, flood, or snowstorm. The newspaper reports the latest police news. The cell phone updates the terrorist level. The neighbor reports on the breakup of the couple around the corner. Before we know it, we're suffocating under a barrage of bad news.

Take a break. Put the TV on mute. Shut off the radio. Forget about the weather. Recycle the paper. Power down your phone. Shut your front door. And watch a comedy show or movie that gives you genuine belly laughs. Allow God's gift of laughter to heal you, to lift you out of your stress and into His holy joy. Get yourself a godly guffaw!

Lord, I'm stuck in a bad-news rut.
Help me to hone in on Your healing joy.

Faith, Love, and Hope

We give thanks to God always for all of you, constantly mentioning you in our prayers, remembering before our God and Father your work of faith and labor of love and steadfastness of hope in our Lord Jesus Christ.

1 Thessalonians 1:2–3 esv

The prayers of those who have gone before us are continually before God (see Revelation 5:8; 8:3). And the prayers of our loved ones stick to us like gum on a hot sidewalk. As Abraham Lincoln said, "I remember my mother's prayers and they have always followed me. They have clung to me all my life."

Not only do you have the prayer power to cover your own loved ones, but saints, such as the apostle Paul, have used their prayer power to cover you. Be encouraged by this. Know that because of your faith, great things are happening and will happen in your life. That others are grateful for your labors in love.

Relax and tap into the timelessness of faith, love, and hope.

*Thank You, Jesus, for the faith, love,
and hope with which You bless me.*

Straighten Up

For God is not a God of disorder but of peace.
1 CORINTHIANS 14:33 NLT

You have a commitment on Saturday, a birthday party for a little one. You have the gift, the gift bag, and the card but can't find the invitation. You're too embarrassed to call the hostess and ask what time you're supposed to show up. So you spend three days tearing your house apart. You finally call another friend who's going, hoping she hasn't lost her invitation. She hasn't. She gives you the show-up time and you do just that. The following Monday, you find your invitation under a pile of papers on your desk. Argh!

Has this, or something similar, ever happened to you? If so, it's time to straighten up your purse, desk, office, house. Doing so will keep you from suffering from disorderly stress and open up your days with some orderly peace.

Help me, Lord, to stop and straighten up my life
every once in a while. I know doing so will be
time spent in a worthy pursuit of peace.

See the Trees

*Ask the birds of the air, and let them tell you; or speak to
the earth [with its many forms of life], and it will teach you;
and let the fish of the sea declare [this truth] to you.*
JOB 12:7–8 AMP

God wants you out and about, looking at His creation, learning
its lessons, breathing in its beauty, praising its presence, allowing it to speak. Amazingly enough, looking at trees—the more
the better—will relieve your stress! Both exercising amid the
boughs and just looking at them will lower your blood pressure and lift your mood. What an amazing God you have, who
has given you a simple way to lower your stress.

Whether you live in the city or the country, find a tree or
three or more. Beat a path to a forest floor. Or simply stare at
some trees from your window. Take a few deep belly breaths.
Praise God for the trees' beauty and power to lift your spirits.
See the trees and ease the stress.

Thank You, Lord, for the tranquility of Your trees.

Are You There?

*Let us also lay aside every weight. . .looking to Jesus,
the founder and perfecter of our faith.*
HEBREWS 12:1–2 ESV

During Jesus' time on earth, no matter what was happening in His life, no matter how many people were vying for His attention, He kept His eyes on His Father. He went alone to a quiet place where He could get calm, focus, and spend time in the company of the Master Creator. This time of solitude and single-minded devotion allowed Him to come away refreshed, rejuvenated, replenished, ready to give His entire attention to those who came to Him.

Are you there for Jesus? Are you there for God? Are you there for others? Are you even there for yourself?

Unplug yourself from the world—including your phone, computer, TV, and radio—a few times a week, at least. Plug into God, Jesus, the Spirit. Spend time with the Creator and His creation. Then use that energy and power to plug into yourself and those around you. Focus, be fed, then feed. Be there.

*Lord, help me to be there for You, myself, and others.
Be the reigning power in my life once again!*

Let Loose

David was dancing before the LORD with great enthusiasm. . . .
So David and all the house of Israel were bringing the
ark of the LORD up [to the City of David] with shouts
[of joy] and with the sound of the trumpet.
2 SAMUEL 6:14–15 AMP

There's a time to dance—either before, during, or after stressful situations. Try it. Why? Because dancing helps to de-stress you. Regardless of how well you do it, dancing releases endorphins, which make your body feel better and improve your mind's outlook, making you feel calmer and more optimistic. Even better is the fact that music, whether you're playing, dancing to, or listening to it, lowers pulse and heart rates, blood pressure, and stress hormone levels.

So let loose. Dance before the Lord. Praise Him with music and song. Pick up an instrument and play for Him. Before you know it, you'll be bringing joy to God and yourself!

I am so grateful for the power of music, Lord. Let's dance!

Bringing Out the Best

"I'm telling you to love your enemies. Let them bring out the best in you, not the worst. When someone gives you a hard time, respond with the energies of prayer, for then you are working out of your true selves, your God-created selves."
MATTHEW 5:44–45 MSG

There are those authorities who tell you to stay away from people who frustrate you, who stress you out. But Jesus tells you to pray for them. To love them.

Inspirational writer William Arthur Ward has a wonderful maxim to live by: "When we seek to discover the best in others, we somehow bring out the best in ourselves."

Keep these thoughts in mind the next time you come across a relative or acquaintance, a coworker or fellow church member who brings out the fight, flight, or freeze response in you. Look for the best in that person. And see what happens within your own self.

*Lord, help me to continually love and look
for the best in everyone, as You do me.*

Go Deep

*Why are you in despair, O my soul? And why have you
become restless and disturbed within me? Hope in
God and wait expectantly for Him, for I shall again
praise Him for the help of His presence.*
PSALM 42:5 AMP

What do you do when moments of stress come on suddenly
and there's nowhere to run and hide?

It's in those moments you need to recognize that all you're
doing is facing a moment of stress. There's no real immediate
danger. Take a deep breath and remember that God has promised
never to leave you or forsake you. Although you don't have
a physical quiet place to retreat to, you can meet God in the
quiet place of your heart. Allow your spirit to go deep, to call
to and be answered by the Holy Spirit within. Know His song
is with you.

*Help me to practice going deep with You,
Lord, so I'll react with peace in You—
within and without—no matter where I am.*

Decisions, Decisions

*Such things were written in the Scriptures long ago to teach us.
And the Scriptures give us hope and encouragement as
we wait patiently for God's promises to be fulfilled.*
ROMANS 15:4 NLT

Even the easiest of decisions can seem difficult at times, especially when many different choices are available to us. So what's a woman to do to receive good and godly guidance every day?

Spend time with God, an open Bible upon your lap. Before reading the scriptures, let your prayer be something like this:

Lord, tell me what You want me to know.
Show me what You want me to see.
Lead me where You want me to go.
Make me what You want me to be.

Then rest assured that God will give you the wisdom to make the right decision in His eyes.

*I know You will give me all the wisdom I desire,
Lord. Walk with me. Talk to me. I await
Your direction with patience and trust.*

Caught Up

*Simon answered, "Master, we toiled all night and took
nothing! But at your word I will let down the nets."
And when they had done this, they enclosed a large
number of fish, and their nets were breaking.*
LUKE 5:5–6 ESV

Sometimes we get so caught up in our lives, so stressed out,
that we don't recognize where God may be directing our attention, the solutions He might be providing if only we'd look or
listen, whether through circumstances, prayer, the wisdom of
others, or the scriptures.

Consider how Jesus was preaching one day from Simon's boat
after a long night of unsuccessful fishing on the part of Simon
and his crew. Yet at Jesus' word, Simon lowered his nets—and
brought up a bounty of fish.

Are you awake and open to what God is saying? Where
might He be telling you to let down your net?

*Lord, I come before You, my eyes and ears open.
What would You have me do?*

Patiently Ponder in Prayer

Mary was keeping within herself all these things (sayings),
weighing and pondering them in her heart.
LUKE 2:19 AMPC

Events you never foresaw are happening all around you. There is so much going on, so much commotion in your world and life that your thoughts are pitter-pattering like so many raindrops splashing onto a tin roof. You begin losing sleep in the night hours, wondering what will happen next or how you can keep what you think is going to happen from happening. In the daytime, your judgment becomes skewed. You have so many thoughts careening around in your head, you can no longer take information in.

What's missing in your life? Patiently pondering in prayer, trusting that God is with you and will reveal things in His own good time. As Mother Teresa said, "Prayer is not asking. Prayer is putting oneself in the hands of God, at His disposition, and listening to His voice in the depths of our hearts."

Lord, help me to pray, ponder, and put myself
in Your hands as You speak to my heart.

Rest versus Stress

Stand by the roads and look; and ask for the eternal paths, where the good, old way is; then walk in it, and you will find rest for your souls. But they said, We will not walk in it!
JEREMIAH 6:16 AMPC

Have a decision to make? A path to choose? Looking for direction? For peace? God has all the answers for you and even outlines them in Jeremiah 6:16. Step 1: Stand where you are and look around. Consider all the possible options. Step 2: Pray. Ask God for His good way. Step 3: Walk in it. Now that you know the right way (through praying for wisdom, heeding God's voice, and using the Bible as your road map), you will find rest for your soul.

You could also choose (a) to do none of those things or (b) to refuse to walk in the path God has laid out for you. Both of those options lead to stress.

So stop. Stand by, now, in this moment. Take steps 1 through 3. Choose rest, not stress.

I'm at the crossroads, Lord, looking for Your way.

Perception

The LORD said to Samuel, "Don't judge by his appearance
or height, for I have rejected him. The LORD doesn't see
things the way you see them. People judge by outward
appearance, but the LORD looks at the heart."

1 SAMUEL 16:7 NLT

Stress often comes to the fore when we think we need to and do
have all the answers. When we think that what we perceive is
indeed the true and only reality. But God turns that idea upside
down over and over in the Bible, perhaps most notably when
the prophet Samuel looked to secretly anoint one of Jesse's eight
sons as the next king. He began with the oldest and ended up
with David, the youngest and smallest of Jesse's boys. Selecting
him went against all logic, all human sense and reasoning. But
Samuel obeyed.

God sees so much more than you do. Your role is to seek His
knowledge, let Him have His say, then do as He wills, regardless
of how much sense it makes to you.

Help me, Lord, to seek and be open to
Your vision in every situation I face.

God's Own Heart

"God removed Saul and replaced him with David, a man about whom God said, 'I have found David son of Jesse, a man after my own heart. He will do everything I want him to do.' "
ACTS 13:22 NLT

So many rules are out there. And they've been around for years. Look at all the rules the Pharisees made and insisted the Jews follow. Trying to follow them was most likely unbelievably stressful.

Fortunately, God makes things simple for those who follow Christ. He wants you to be a God-follower more than just a rule-follower. All you have to do is listen and obey. Make His will yours. You can begin by loving God with all your heart, mind, body, spirit, soul, and strength. And then love others as yourself.

Let the stress and unnecessary rules fall away. Become a woman after God's own heart.

Lord, help me be a woman who follows the Rule Giver more than the rules. Help me to be a woman after Your own heart.

Creative Endeavor

Then you will seek Me, inquire for, and require Me
[as a vital necessity] and find Me when you
search for Me with all your heart.
JEREMIAH 29:13 AMPC

When we get out of our own heads and into God's head, seeking Him with all our heart, we tap into the creativity of the Creator. Possibilities abound. Ideas become limitless. His answers are often surprising, things we never thought of. The stress melts away as solutions pour down.

There's no need to think this heart-avenue is blocked, not open to you, that you are ill-equipped. For God says in Jeremiah 24:7 (ESV): "I will give them a heart to know that I am the LORD, and they shall be my people and I will be their God, for they shall return to me with their whole heart."

So what are you waiting for? Allow prayer to be your creative and limitless endeavor. Go to God. Seek Him with your whole heart, and He will expand your world.

I come to You, Lord, with my whole heart.

Meditative Reflection

Let the words of my mouth and the meditation
of my heart be acceptable in Your sight, O Lord,
my [firm, impenetrable] Rock and my Redeemer.
PSALM 19:14 AMPC

Philosopher Denis Diderot said, "There are three principal means of acquiring knowledge. . .observation of nature, reflection, and experimentation. Observation collects facts; reflection combines them; and experimentation verifies the result of that combination."

The more knowledge you have of God, the more you find yourself trusting Him and the less you stress. It's easy enough to observe Him, to collect facts about Him. But do you reflect on those facts? Do you allow them to bring you deeper into His arms? Do you open up and give Him access to your heart, so that He can come in and sup with you, lead you, love you? Do you incorporate your observations and reflections into your life, bringing God even more into your "reality"?

Consider these things. Then use them to grow deeper into your Rock and Redeemer.

Lord, make my meditation such that I
would learn to know and love You more.

The Son Is Still There

Fix your thoughts on what is true, and honorable,
and right, and pure, and lovely, and admirable.
Think about things that are excellent and worthy of praise.
PHILIPPIANS 4:8 NLT

The apostle Paul had experienced his share of sickness, hunger, imprisonment, persecution, and more. He knew how easy it was for Jesus' followers to get stressed out, hung up on all the hazards of their faith facing them. But he also knew the secret of getting out from under all the negative news. His own rule and his advice to readers was to think about the good things.

Pay attention to what's running through your head. Fix your thoughts on higher things. As Gloria Gaither said, "Even in the winter, in the midst of the storm, the sun is still there. Somewhere above the clouds, it still shines and warms and pulls at the life buried deep inside the brown branches and frozen earth."

Help me, Lord, to remember to keep my thoughts on good
things, like You, to rise above the stresses and into Your light.

Lessons to Learn

"As it is written in the Scriptures, 'They will all be taught by God.' Everyone who listens to the Father and learns from him comes to me."
JOHN 6:45 NLT

Ralph Waldo Emerson said, "No man ever prayed heartily without learning something."

What is your prayer life like? Do you take the things that are stressing you out and present them to God? Do you put your entire heart into the endeavor? Do you ask God to show you what He wants you to see before you open up His Word? Are you persistently asking, seeking, and knocking on His door (see Matthew 7:7)? Are you allowing yourself to be vulnerable, letting Him into your world—heart, mind, body, spirit, and soul—opening the door where He is seeking entry (see Revelation 3:20)?

God has good things in store for you, wisdom to impart, words to heal, love to give, lessons to learn. Look. Listen. Learn.

Lord, I come before You, seeking You with my entire being. Teach me what You would have me know. In Jesus' name. Amen.

Time-Out

*The Sovereign Lord. . .says: "Only in returning to me
and resting in me will you be saved. In quietness and
confidence is your strength." . . . Your own ears will hear
him. Right behind you a voice will say, "This is the way
you should go," whether to the right or to the left.*
Isaiah 30:15, 21 nlt

When a child gets a time-out from her parents, she may find
herself in a chair by herself, perhaps facing a wall. It's quiet with
no distractions at hand. No toys, books, TV, or radio allowed.
The period of sequestering is usually one minute for each year
of age, during which time the child has time to reflect and rest.
At the end, she's ready to go again—hopefully the right way.

When was the last time you took time out with God, returned
to Him, rested in Him, and came away quieter within and, having
heard Him speak, more confident in Him? Try a time-out with
God today. The length is up to you—and Him.

Lord, I'm returning for rest in You today.

An Ensouled Being

So those who received his word were baptized, and there
were added that day about three thousand souls. And
they devoted themselves to the apostles' teaching and the
fellowship, to the breaking of bread and the prayers.
And awe came upon every soul.
ACTS 2:41–43 ESV

C. S. Lewis said, "We don't have a soul. We are a soul. We happen to have a body."

How would your life change if you looked at it from the perspective of your being a soul that just happens to be inhabiting a body? According to HELPS Word-studies, the word *soul* used in the verses above corresponds to the Old Testament word for "soul": "The soul is the direct aftermath of God breathing (blowing) His gift of life into a person, making them an *ensouled being*" (emphasis added).

See yourself as an eternal creature who has been given God's breath of life, who has been endowed with a soul, and you'll find yourself more awed than anxious.

I am Your breath within a body, Lord.
Help me to live Your way.

Always and All Ways

God is our refuge and strength, a very present help in trouble.
Therefore we will not fear though the earth gives way,
though the mountains be moved into the heart of the sea.
PSALM 46:1–2 ESV

The author of Psalm 46 would have you remember a very calming fact: God is there for you, right beside you, a fortress to which you can run and hide, your very strength in times of trouble—no matter what that trouble is, where it is happening, or to whom it is happening. Because of that fact, there really is no reason to stress or strain. As the psalmist goes on to explain, there is absolutely nothing that God cannot handle, no tide He cannot turn, no fire He cannot quench, no lion He cannot tame. Remember this truth.

God says, "Be still, and know that I am God" (Psalm 46:10 ESV). *You* are not. But *He* is. And He is with you—always and in all ways.

Thank You, Lord, for being the one and
only true God. Help me to be still in You.

Inclined to Pray

"Incline your ear, O LORD, and hear;
open your eyes, O LORD, and see."
2 KINGS 19:16 ESV

Talk about being stressed. King Hezekiah and his kingdom of Judah were being threatened at the gates, and his God was being bad-mouthed by the very powerful king of Assyria who then put his threats and insults in a letter to Hezekiah.

But Hezekiah didn't freak out. He went to God and spread the letter before Him. Then he prayed, praising God for all His power. Asking Him to hear and see what was happening in his life. Asking God to save him—so that everyone would see that He alone was God.

The result? "That night the angel of the LORD went out and struck down 185,000 in the camp of the Assyrians. . . . Then Sennacherib king of Assyria departed" (2 Kings 19:35–36 ESV).

If God could do this for Hezekiah, imagine what He can do for you!

Lord, I know You are amazing. Hear and see me.
Help me, so that all will know You alone are God!

Close to His Heart

He will feed his flock like a shepherd. He will carry
the lambs in his arms, holding them close to his heart.
ISAIAH 40:11 NLT

You are in the Great Shepherd's arms. You have no need to fear.
To struggle. To panic. You are in the safest place you could ever
be. In the arms of the One who loves you beyond compare,
who sacrificed His life so that you could be with Him forever.
He is watching over you. He's the barrier between you and that
which could harm you. He is the One who meets all your needs.
He leads you down the right paths, to clean, living water and
food that satisfies.

So be still. Relax in His arms. Lean back. Breathe deep. Feel
His heartbeat. You are home. Let Him carry you.

Lord, here I am, leaning back against You, listening to
Your heartbeat, feeling Your breath and the warmth of
Your love. Hold me tight. Keep me close forevermore.

Everything Will Be Fine

The LORD replied, "I will personally go with you. . .
and I will give you rest—everything will be fine for you."
EXODUS 33:14 NLT

Whenever she heard concern in an adult's voice or saw a furrowed brow, three-year-old Emmaleen would respond with, "It'll be fine." Over and over again, she blessed the lives and calmed the qualms of many with her little mantra, "It'll be fine." How did she arrive at this conclusion? How did it become such a big part of her own life and personality as the years went by? These three little words were the same ones Emmaleen's mother often imparted to her.

God wants you to get the same message, repeat the same mantra, know the same truth. That no matter what has happened, is happening, or might happen, God is with you. He is personally at your side. He will give you rest. "Everything will be fine for you."

Help me to have the faith and trust of a
three-year-old, Lord. Help me to see that
with You right next to me, it'll be fine.

Your Very Breath

They should seek God, in the hope that they might feel after Him and find Him, although He is not far from each one of us. For in Him we live and move and have our being.
ACTS 17:27–28 AMPC

God is not some distant, foreign deity. He is closer than your very breath. St. Gregory of Nazianzus advised us, "Remember God more often than you breathe."

Imagine thinking of God with each inhale and exhale. Pause in this moment and feel that breath. Feel God's presence. Recognize He is above, below, within, and without. With these ideas at the forefront of your mind and the awareness of His love in the depths of your soul, there is no room for fight, flight, or freeze. Simply peace as you live, move, and have your being.

Lord, You are not some piece of wood or stone. You are a living God who is working in my life, taking care of me, and bringing me peace and contentment in this very moment as I live and breathe. In Jesus' name. Amen.

Breaking Chains

Paul and Silas were praying and singing hymns to God. . . .
Suddenly, there was a massive earthquake, and the prison
was shaken to its foundations. All the doors immediately
flew open, and the chains of every prisoner fell off!
ACTS 16:25–26 NLT

"Prayer is not only worship; it is also an invisible emanation of man's worshiping spirit—the most powerful form of energy that one can generate," wrote Nobel Prize winner Alexis Carrel, MD.

Prayer is a force that can shake open doors, make chains fall away, and set prisoners free. With all this power, prayer obviously can release your stress, make your burdens fall away, and change your limited perspective. All you need to do is believe it is possible. When you do, you will be singing with the chorus, "Our Lord is great, with limitless strength" (Psalm 147:5 MSG).

I want to tap into Your power, Lord. I know nothing
is too hard or impossible for You. Help me to have
a strong prayer life that breaks chains.

Steer Clear

He drew me up out of a horrible pit [a pit of tumult and of destruction], out of the miry clay (froth and slime), and set my feet upon a rock, steadying my steps and establishing my goings.
PSALM 40:2 AMPC

God has a threefold process to get you up out of the pit of needless stress. First, He'll pull you to safety. Then He'll set your feet on solid ground and help you find your balance again, giving you security. Finally, He'll guide you to the next venture, helping you steer clear of future pitfalls. Afterward, you'll be singing a new tune, praising God. Others will notice what's happening in your life and find themselves wanting what you have and trusting more in the Lord.

The only thing you need to do is reach out to Him. Let Him know what's going on in your life. He will listen. He will see. He will reach down and lift you up to safety, give you the security you crave, and help you steer clear of snags.

I'm so ready, Lord. Pull me up to You!

Holding Nothing Back

*GOD met me more than halfway, he freed me from my
anxious fears. Look at him; give him your warmest smile.
Never hide your feelings from him. When I was desperate,
I called out, and GOD got me out of a tight spot.*
PSALM 34:4–6 MSG

Hannah is a great example of how to approach God in prayer.
While under great stress, and having already cried a river of
tears, Hannah went to the temple. She "was in distress of soul,
praying to the Lord and weeping bitterly" (1 Samuel 1:10 AMPC).
She told God everything! She made promises and continued
praying before Him silently—"speaking in her heart; only her
lips moved but her voice was not heard" (1 Samuel 1:13 AMPC).

God hears your prayers, whether said aloud or silently. And
when you look to Him for help, baring your heart to Him, He
will meet you more than halfway. He'll free you from stress and
fear. He'll rescue you. What are you waiting for?

*Lord, I pour out my heart to You right now,
holding nothing back. Free me!*

Circle of Protection

GOD's angel sets up a circle of protection around us while we pray. Open your mouth and taste, open your eyes and see—how good GOD is. Blessed are you who run to him. Worship GOD if you want the best; worship opens doors to all his goodness.

PSALM 34:7–9 MSG

Amid a stressful situation in which you see no way out—mentally, physically, emotionally, spiritually—go to God. As soon as you're in His presence, He'll set up, between you and whatever's coming against you, a protective barrier. See it. Know it's there. Do not doubt. Then open your mouth and pray. Realize how good God is. Praise Him for what He's doing in your life. Know that even if you still don't see a way out, that's okay. You're with the Master Planner and Protector. He's got you covered. He has an exit plan. He has good things lined up and coming your way. Then rest in His peace.

I see no way out of this, Lord, but I know You do.
And in You I trust. In You I have peace.

Catch Your Breath

Is anyone crying for help? GOD is listening, ready to rescue
you. If your heart is broken, you'll find GOD right there; if
you're kicked in the gut, he'll help you catch your breath.
Disciples so often get into trouble; still, GOD is there every time.
PSALM 34:17–19 MSG

The word *stress* has an interesting etymology, coming in part
from words meaning "narrowness," "oppression," and "drawn
tight." So it makes sense that when you're under stress you
may feel as if the walls are closing in on you. As if your chest
is drawn tight. It's almost hard to breathe.

On the one hand, there is stress, a sense of suffocation. On
the other hand, there is God. The key is to remember God in the
midst of your stress. To remember He is listening and ready to
rescue you, to help you catch your breath. He'll do it every time.
His job is to be there for you. Your job is to reach out for Him.

Help me to catch my breath, Lord!

Bold Soul

I give you thanks, O LORD, with my whole heart. . . .
On the day I called, you answered me;
my strength of soul you increased.
PSALM 138:1, 3 ESV

Consider the fact that on the day you call on God, He answers you. Open yourself up to the idea that as soon as you cry out, He responds, just as a breastfeeding mother automatically—physically, mentally, emotionally—responds to the cry of her newborn, ready to succor her little one at the first sign of hunger.

That's how God responds to you. He not only answers you but gives you so much strength in your soul that you are emboldened, able to overcome the fight, flight, and freeze reactions. He gives you the power to let go of worldly anxiety, replacing stress with His strength and boldness of spirit.

Call. He'll respond and give you all the strength you need. Then thank Him with your whole heart.

You amaze me, Lord, with how quickly You respond
to my cry. I thank You for giving me strength!

Safe and Sound

No one stood by me. They all ran like scared rabbits.
But it doesn't matter—the Master stood by me and
helped me. . . . God's looking after me, keeping me
safe in the kingdom of heaven.
2 TIMOTHY 4:16–18 MSG

Are you aware of God's care all the time? Do you know that no matter what troubles you step in the middle of, He won't leave you alone? He has a long and loving reach. There is nothing He cannot turn around to work for your good. You may not see it now, but that's okay. You will someday. He has His hand on you. His love and protection are never-ending.

So take heart. God is working out all plans in your favor. Just continue hoping, trusting, praying. Your deliverer is right next to you, standing by you, keeping you safe and sound!

Lord, one thing that keeps me going is knowing I'm not alone.
You are forever with me, loving me, helping me, rescuing me.

Looks Are Everything

Seeing Peter and John about to go into the temple, he asked to receive alms. And Peter directed his gaze at him, as did John, and said, "Look at us." And he fixed his attention on them, expecting to receive something from them.

ACTS 3:3–5 ESV

How do you begin your day? With a sense of helplessness and hopelessness? Are you looking for signs that somehow you'll eke out something good? Or are you fixing your attention on Jesus, expecting that He'll give you something beyond the best?

The beggar outside the temple thought he knew what he needed and that money was what Peter and John would give him. When told to look at them, the beggar did so, "expecting to receive something." What he got was something much more valuable than silver or gold. He received the power of Jesus Christ working in his life.

Put no limits on God. Simply look to Jesus and expect beyond the best!

As I begin this day, Lord, I'm looking for You and Your power to do something amazing in my life. My eyes are fixed on You!

Aiming to Please and Praise

She said, "This time I'll praise GOD."
So she named him Judah (Praise-GOD).
GENESIS 29:35 MSG

Sometimes women get stressed out looking for love, recognition, contentment, and satisfaction in all the wrong places. Leah, knowing her husband Jacob had been tricked into marrying her, did all she could to win at least a portion of Jacob's love away from her barren sister Rachel. Leah named her firstborn Reuben (See, it's a boy!), thinking that effort would make Jacob love her. The second she named Simeon, as she realized God had heard her prayers. The third she named Levi, companion, thinking now Jacob would connect with her. Finally, she had Judah, saying, "Now I'll praise God."

Amid our prayerful expectations, we would be wise to acknowledge, thank, and praise God for the comfort He continually gives us, even when our prayers are not answered exactly as we'd hoped, for the Lord alone should be the One we aim to please and praise in our lives.

I praise You, Lord, for all You have
done and are doing in my life!

From Stress to Strength

This is my prayer. That God. . .will give you spiritual wisdom and the insight to know more of him: that you may receive that inner illumination of the spirit which will make you realise how great is the hope to which he is calling you. . .and how tremendous is the power available to us who believe in God.
EPHESIANS 1:17–19 PHILLIPS

Within you lies all the power required to turn your stress into strength and, in turn, turn your mourning into dancing (see Psalm 30:11). But first you have to believe that the same power that resurrected Jesus is alive and working in you! That it's unlimited, unassailable, unbelievable!

Thousands of years ago, the apostle Paul prayed that God would give you spiritual wisdom and insight to know Him better and realize the amazing power available to you.

Look for it. Express it. Move out of your stress and into God's strength—and dance.

With Your Spirit within me, Lord, I can do all You've called me to do. Keep this fact before me as I move from stress to strength.

Mind of Plenty

*Every beast of the forest is Mine, and the cattle upon a
thousand hills or upon the mountains where thousands are.*
PSALM 50:10 AMPC

It's exhausting vying to buy the most and the best this world
has to offer, all we think we are entitled to, trying to assuage
the desperate feeling of not having enough. But this idea of lack
is not put into us by God.

God constantly tells us of the plenty surrounding us. He
knows exactly what we need and will provide it (see Matthew
6:25–33). Not that we aren't supposed to work. Even the apostle
Paul was a tentmaker. The point is not to stress ourselves out
trying to buy the most and the best. The point is to approach
life with a mind-set not of lack but of plenty, sharing what we
have when we can (see Luke 3:11) and working with all our
heart, as if we're working for the Lord (see Colossians 3:23),
the One with cattle upon a thousand hills, knowing He will
not fail to provide.

*Lord, help me to change my mind-set
from my lack to Your plenty.*

From Stress to Stillness

*God did not give us a spirit of timidity (of cowardice,
of craven and cringing and fawning fear), but [He has
given us a spirit] of power and of love and of calm and
well-balanced mind and discipline and self-control.*
2 TIMOTHY 1:7 AMPC

Corrie ten Boom wrote, "Worry is a cycle of inefficient thoughts whirling around a center of fear." And once that whirling begins, it can grow to pull in every other thought that touches it, making your entire being spin out of control and be overtaken by stress.

The remedy is to remember God didn't give you a spirit of fear but of power, love, and calm. In Him your mind is well balanced. And as you become more aware of your thoughts, taking every one of them captive and turning them over to Christ, the waters settle. When we put God's truth up against the false worries that tend to drown us out, we find ourselves back with our Shepherd, beside the still waters.

Thank You, Lord, for the spirit of power and calm in You.

Change Your Outlook

Jesus called a little child to his side. . . . "Believe me," he said,
"unless you change your whole outlook and become like little
children you will never enter the kingdom of Heaven."
MATTHEW 18:2–3 PHILLIPS

Take this moment to check in with yourself. What's your outlook? Are you seeing this world as a hard place to exist, wondering when the next proverbial shoe will drop? Are you expecting the clouds instead of the sun?

Imagine being a small, innocent child with no agenda, one who trusts, loves, forgives easily, and has no ego. Imagine holding Jesus' hand, knowing He's your big brother, the One who will keep you safe, feed you, lead you, help you, lift you up. As you hold on to His hand, imagine walking by His side. The world is a wonderland as you walk through it, curious as to what you will find, what gifts you will uncover.

Hold on to that hand. Change your outlook. Become God's child.

God of my heart and soul, hold my hand.
Lead me. I am but Your child.

Walking in Rhythm

"May he [God] keep us centered and devoted to him, following the life path he has cleared, watching the signposts, walking at the pace and rhythms he laid down for our ancestors."
1 KINGS 8:58 MSG

When we are walking out of step with God, stress can seep into our lives. Where might you be off center? How might you have stepped off the path God has laid out for you? What distractions have kept you from watching for, seeing, and reading the signposts He has planted for you throughout your journey? How can you get out of the rhythm of this walk you have set out on and get back to God's pace for your life?

Spend some time taking an inventory of your activities, priorities, goals. Go to God in prayer and ask where your priorities might differ from His. Then begin revising your stride to keep pace with His rhythm on His good path.

Lord, I come to You, looking to set my pace with Yours.

Recognition

Now when they saw the boldness of Peter and John, and perceived that they were uneducated, common men, they were astonished. And they recognized that they had been with Jesus.
ACTS 4:13 ESV

Sometimes the symptoms of stress can be quite obvious—low energy, nervousness, loss of focus, sleeplessness, weakness, timidity, jumpiness, tenseness, etc.—all of which keep others (and ourselves, perhaps) from recognizing that we have been with Jesus. For His persona exudes the exact opposite characteristics. Jesus is tireless, calm, focused, rested, bold, peaceful, and relaxed.

Spend time each day with Jesus. When you do, His characteristics will rub off on you bit by bit. Each day you will become more like Him until one day, people will look at you and recognize you have spent time in the presence of Jesus.

At this point, Jesus, I'm not sure what—or who— people see when they look at me. So I'm coming to spend time with You, imbibing Your peace, strength, boldness, and so much more. May I grow each day to look more like You than anything or anyone else.

Her Part, His Part

"Now, Lord. . .grant to your servants to continue to speak your word with all boldness, while you stretch out your hand to heal, and signs and wonders are performed through the name of your holy servant Jesus." And when they had prayed. . .they were all filled with the Holy Spirit and continued to speak the word of God with boldness.
ACTS 4:29–31 ESV

Feeling as if the whole world is on your shoulders? Thinking if you don't do it, it won't get done? Stop and consider that those feelings and thoughts are lies. For you have a God who is in it with you all the way. In fact, He wants you to know there are two parts to consider in your life—yours and His.

Your part is to immerse yourself in God's Word, pray, welcome His Spirit, expect the Lord is acting on your behalf, and leave the results to Him. His part is to work wonders.

*Lord, help me to do what You would
have me do and leave the rest to You.*

No Distractions

Josiah. . .began his thirty-one-year reign in Jerusalem. . . .
He did right in the sight of the Lord. . .and turned
not aside to the right hand or to the left.
2 KINGS 22:1–2 AMPC

Josiah was one of the best kings of Judah because he did not allow himself to turn aside from God's calling on his life.

When we're moving along on the path God has called us to, it's easy to get distracted by things along the way. When we do, we begin losing ground on what we're supposed to be doing, where we're supposed to be going. Falling ever further behind, we feel the stress of not being where we're supposed to be, and it begins to overwhelm us.

Look to what may be in your path. Then consider living by the wisdom of Proverbs 4:25–27 (MSG): "Keep your eyes straight ahead; ignore all sideshow distractions. Watch your step, and the road will stretch out smooth before you. Look neither right nor left."

Help me to steer clear of distractions, Lord,
and keep my feet firmly on Your path.

Tides of the Mind

*Now ask and keep on asking and you will receive, so that
your joy (gladness, delight) may be full and complete.*
JOHN 16:24 AMPC

Poet and suffragist Alice Meynell wrote, "Happiness is not a
matter of events; it depends upon the tides of the mind." If you've
been looking for happiness in other people or circumstances to
no avail, Jesus has your answer. He can help you to have joy in
any situation if you simply ask Him to help you navigate the
tides of your mind, keeping life events from becoming major
stressors.

If you miss the bus, send up a prayer, then look around to
see what God might want you to do. Perhaps you now have
time for devotions, could help a fellow traveler get a coffee, or
could give your warm scarf to a homeless person. In other words,
find your joy in every life event. See every event and seeming
setback as neither good nor bad but rather as a chance to pray
and see the opportunity God is presenting you.

*Control the tides of my mind, Lord,
so my joy will be in You alone.*

A Matter of Course

*"So don't worry and don't keep saying, 'What shall
we eat. . .drink or. . .wear?'. . . Set your heart on
the kingdom and his goodness, and all these things
will come to you as a matter of course."*
MATTHEW 6:31, 33 PHILLIPS

So many people are stressed out because they put more value
and priority on those things that give them a monetary reward.
In other words, they put work before time with relatives,
children, spouses, friends—even God. They have, as playwright
Arthur Miller put it, been "seduced into thinking that that
which does not make a profit is without value."

Jesus tells us that the most valuable thing we can do is
seek Him and His kingdom above all else. Then we will be
given all those other things we need. Consider your priorities
today. Have you made time for God, secure in the knowledge
that everything else will fall into place once He's number one
in your life?

*Lord, I'm here, seeking You above all else.
My new course is to set my heart on You.*

Imprint on Christ

Throw off your old sinful nature and your former way of life,
which is corrupted by lust and deception. Instead, let the Spirit
renew your thoughts and attitudes. Put on your new nature,
created to be like God—truly righteous and holy.
EPHESIANS 4:22–24 NLT

Young birds follow the first moving thing they see, thinking it's
their mother. This process is called imprinting. And it's the same
process that you, a new creature in Christ, should be following.
Now that your spirit has been reborn, now that you have a new
nature, you are not to stress out while living in this world but
to let God's Spirit renew your mind-set as you follow Jesus.

Throw off the angst and put on Christ's peace. Let go of
sorrow and reach out for His joy. Look away from your lack
and focus on His abundance. Release all doubts and cling to
your faith. Exchange your impatience with His patience. Erase
all stress as you imprint on Christ.

You, Jesus, are my Brother. May I become
more and more like You every day.

The Healing Word

*My child, pay attention to what I say. Listen carefully
to my words. Don't lose sight of them. Let them penetrate
deep into your heart, for they bring life to those who
find them, and healing to their whole body.*
PROVERBS 4:20–22 NLT

Too much stress, worry, and strain can cause you physical
damage, not to mention emotional, psychological, mental, and
spiritual harm. But God's Word can heal all that.

Make it a daily endeavor to delve into God's Word. If you
have a good half hour, soak in His wisdom. If you have less
than that, even only one minute, ask God to show you what
He would have you know today. Then open your Bible or
devotional. Uncover a verse that speaks to you. Focus on its
content, intent, and portent. Ask God how it applies to your
life, and acknowledge that it's feeding and healing your whole
self, leading you from feeling stressed to feeling blessed.

*Thank You, God, for feeding me,
healing me with the power of Your Word.*

Faithful Investment

*"'Well done!' the king exclaimed. 'You are a good servant.
You have been faithful with the little I entrusted to you.'"*
LUKE 19:17 NLT

Before going on a long trip, a nobleman divides ten pounds
of silver between three servants, saying, "Invest this for me
while I am gone" (verse 13 NLT). When the nobleman returns
as king, the first servant reports he invested his portion of
the master's money and increased it tenfold. The second says
his investment increased fivefold. Both of these servants are
rewarded according to how they profited. But the last servant,
who, fearing the master, did nothing but hid his master's money
to keep it safe, is stripped of what he was given.

The point is that God wants you to invest the gifts He's
given you but not stress over the results. Your responsibility
is to do only what He asks. Then relax, leaving the results
to Him, and return for further orders, rejoicing over a task
completed in His name.

*Lord, show me how to invest the gifts You've
given me then leave the results to You alone.*

Under the Influence

"Teacher," they said, "we know that you speak and teach what is right and are not influenced by what others think. You teach the way of God truthfully."

LUKE 20:21 NLT

Pastor Harry Emerson Fosdick said, "Prayer is putting yourself under God's influence." To understand this and the above verse better, let's look at the etymology of the word *influence*. According to etymonline.com, *influence* is a late-fourteenth-century astrological term, meaning "streaming ethereal power from the stars when in certain positions, acting upon the character or destiny of men" and also "a flow of water, flowing in."

Stop for a moment. Ask yourself whose influence you are under during most of your day. Then consider how you can put yourself under God's influence 24-7 through prayer. Doing so will keep you from bowing to the influence of society, the media, and so on, and keep your pathway to peace secure.

I'm tired of worrying about what other people think about who I am, what I do. I want You, Lord, to be my one and only influence. Stream Your guiding Spirit upon me.

The Quiet Power of Women

In quietness and in [trusting]
confidence shall be your strength.
ISAIAH 30:15 AMPC

In the British television series *Wycliffe*, Detective Superintendent Charles Wycliffe remarks to his wife, "It's interesting, isn't it, the quiet power of women." That statement is just as true today as it was thousands of years ago.

Consider the fact that men have most of the lines in the Bible. Yet most women, when they do speak, do so with passion and power. Esther suggested a fast for her people then simply said, "If I perish, I perish" (Esther 4:16 ESV). The woman with the issue of blood thought (but did not say), "If I can just touch his robe, I will be healed" (Mark 5:28 NLT). The women standing at the cross said. . .nothing. And in the Garden, when Mary Magdalene realized the supposed gardener was actually Jesus, she said simply, "Teacher!" and then ran to tell the others the good news.

Don't stress. You have a quiet power. Prayer is a part of that power. Stress less, pray more.

Lord, may my confidence in You be my source of quiet power.

Change Agent

*Be careful how you live. . . . Make the most of every
opportunity. . . . Don't act thoughtlessly, but understand
what the Lord wants you to do. . . . Be filled with the Holy
Spirit. . .making music to the Lord in your hearts.*
EPHESIANS 5:15–19 NLT

Want to have some change in your life, live more in God's
world than the one you've created for yourself? Tap into the
power of the Holy Spirit. He's the change agent who will bring
you around to where God desires you to be. He's as close as a
breath, as near as a prayer. He's the gift of the One who loved
you so much He died for you on the cross.

He's not only your Comforter, Counselor, Motivator, and
Life Source. He's the One who'll change your attitude (see
Romans 12:2) and your altitude, drawing you ever closer to
the God of your heart, mind, body, and soul.

*Lord, I'm ready for a change in my life. Help me to handle it,
drawing ever closer to You in the process.*

Slow and Steady

*The thoughts of the [steadily] diligent tend only
to plenteousness, but everyone who is impatient
and hasty hastens only to want.*
PROVERBS 21:5 AMPC

How many times have you felt stressed out because your boss said she needed that report yesterday? How many days a week do you speed from one kid's activity to another then rush home to get dinner on before hubby gets home? How many times have you taken what seemed to be a shortcut but found it actually took you longer to reach your destination?

God wants all things we do to be done in His time, in His rhythm. Proverbs 21:5 (NLT) says that "hasty shortcuts lead to poverty." How can we have a good walk with Jesus if we're always struggling in the yoke that binds us to Him?

First, change your thoughts. Know that God will help you do what needs to be done each day, and the rest will wait. Slow and steady will win the race.

*Lord, help me to slow down in my thoughts and actions,
knowing all things will get done in Your time.*

Natural Rhythm

*"Come to me. Get away with me and you'll recover
your life. I'll show you how to take a real rest.
Walk with me and work with me—watch how I do it.
Learn the unforced rhythms of grace."*
MATTHEW 11:28–30 MSG

Take a moment right now to get away with Jesus. In His presence, you can find, get back, your true life—your life in and with Him. Only He can show you how to take a real break, one that includes His peace, His love, His strength, His nurturing. He is longing for you to take His hand, walk with Him, work with Him, play with Him. Jesus has set you an example, showing you how to spend more time with Father God. How to go up to the mountain alone and pray.

Learn the natural rhythm of God's good grace. He is waiting to show you. Are you willing to learn from Him and turn from the stress that dogs your steps?

*Lord, I'm willing to learn Your rhythm.
Help me to recover my life!*

"Nevertheless. . ."

The Jebusites, the inhabitants of the land. . .said to David,
"You will not come in here, but the blind and the lame will
ward you off"—thinking, "David cannot come in here."
Nevertheless, David took the stronghold of Zion.
2 SAMUEL 5:6–7 ESV

When you have God on your side, there is no need to stress and strain, even when people tell you your efforts will be useless. For God always has a "nevertheless" up His sleeve. His power can work through you when you stay in tune with His Spirit, allowing Him to rule your heart, mind, body, and soul. He will enable you to do above and beyond what you and others think you can do.

Let God's "nevertheless" ease your mind and strengthen your spirit. Know that God will build upon that which you accomplish in His power because, as He was with David, "the God of hosts" (verse 10) is with you.

Lord, help me to see Your "nevertheless" in all the
challenges I face and know that Your power
is with me. In Jesus' name, amen.

At the Center

*Let petitions and praises shape your worries into prayers,
letting God know your concerns. Before you know it, a sense
of God's wholeness, everything coming together for good,
will come and settle you down. It's wonderful what happens
when Christ displaces worry at the center of your life.*
PHILIPPIANS 4:6–7 MSG

When worry overtakes you and stress rears its ugly head, stop
and do a self-check. What's at the center of your life? Who are
you sharing your concerns with? How are you sharing them?

If money, possessions, or people are at the center of your
life, you're bound to stray off course. If you're telling others all
your worries by ranting and raving, those worries become more
powerful, almost taking on a life of their own.

God wants you to come to Him with everything—no
matter how trivial you might think it is. As you pray, pepper
your petitions with praises. Doing so will not only change
your perspective but also give you a sense of God's peace as
Christ "displaces worry at the center of your life."

Let's talk, Lord. Be my center!

Amazing Exchange

In peace I will both lie down and sleep, for You, Lord,
alone make me dwell in safety and confident trust.
PSALM 4:8 AMPC

When we pray before our head hits the pillow—with all our heart, body, mind, soul, and strength—laying all our worries and stressors at God's feet, an amazing exchange takes place. Jesus takes all our problems upon His shoulders and gives us His peace. As we put ourselves in His embrace, He surrounds us with His protection. We are little sheep in the arms of the Great Shepherd, the One who promises to lead us beside still waters and take us to green pastures.

In this way only can we lie down and sleep in peace. For only in His arms, His presence, His light are we truly safe, trusting that as He is with us in the dark night, He will yet be with us in the morning light.

I pray then place myself in Your loving care, Lord.
Watch me through the night.

Thoughts

*"For my thoughts are not your thoughts, neither are your
ways my ways, declares the LORD. For as the heavens
are higher than the earth, so are my ways higher than
your ways and my thoughts than your thoughts."*
ISAIAH 55:8–9 ESV

Every minute of the day we have thoughts going through our
minds, whether or not we're conscious of them. But if we'd
stop in our meanderings and zero in on what we are telling
ourselves (or others), we might find some of our thoughts are
causing us (or others) stress.

God's thoughts aren't our thoughts. He makes that perfectly
clear. But we can change our thoughts to be more like His. We
can renew our minds every morning and throughout the day to
be more like His. We can sing ourselves a new song, one filled
with His promises instead of our problems, His encouragement
instead of our discouragement. Make your thoughts more like
God's and you'll transform your world.

*Lord, help me to become more aware of my thoughts.
Help me to change them up to match Your way of thinking.*

Sinking Stress

"Embrace this God-life. . .and nothing will be too much for you. This mountain, for instance: Just say, 'Go jump in the lake'—no shuffling or shilly-shallying—and it's as good as done. That's why I urge you to pray for absolutely everything."
MARK 11:23–24 MSG

Everyday stressors can turn into mountainous obstacles if we let them. But Jesus has provided a way out for us. He tells us to pray for "absolutely everything" and to put our belief in Him behind our prayers. When we do, when we fully "embrace this God-life," we will find that anything and everything is possible.

So put your wholehearted belief behind God's promises. Claim that nothing is impossible to you who believes (see Mark 9:23). That with God, no one and nothing can stand against you (see Romans 8:31). Speak God's promises to the mountain of stress in front of you. Doing so will pry it loose, lift it up, and toss it into the sea.

I'm wholeheartedly embracing this God-life, Lord! I'm claiming Your promises and watching my stress sink into the sea.

A New Song

Sing God a brand-new song! Earth and
everyone in it, sing! Sing to God—worship God!
PSALM 96:1 MSG

What song was in your head this morning? What might you have been mindlessly humming this afternoon? What might be "playing" in your head this evening? What chorus might you hear when your head hits the pillow?

Homing in on what we're humming and changing up the song can transform our lives. And when we change up that song in our heads to echo one of God's promises or truths, we are, in effect, worshipping our great God.

The most effective way of doing this is to claim each thought. What is it telling you? Does it agree with God's promises or truths? If not, replace it with what God would have you think. In effect, you'll be using God's amazing Word to overpower what the deceiver may have planted in your brain. Here's a general song to help you begin disarming the lies that lead to stress:

"The Lord is my Shepherd [to feed, guide, and shield me],
I shall not lack" [Psalm 23:1 AMPC].

God-Perspective

They brought the Israelites an evil report of the land which they had scouted out, saying, The land through which we went to spy it out is a land that devours its inhabitants.
NUMBERS 13:32 AMPC

Out of the twelve scouts Moses sent into the Promised Land, ten came back with an "evil report," saying, "There we saw the Nephilim. . .who come from the giants; and we were in our own sight as grasshoppers, and so we were in their sight" (verse 33 AMPC). Yet Caleb told the people, "Let us go up at once and possess it; we are well able to conquer it" (verse 30 AMPC).

The first report was evil because those ten scouts had imagined the challenges before them as being bigger than their God! But Caleb, imagining God beside him, knew nothing could defeat them. Because of Caleb's God-perspective, the Lord said, "He has a different spirit; he follows me passionately. I'll bring him into the land that he scouted and his children will inherit it" (Numbers 14:24 MSG).

Help me, Lord, to see You standing beside me in every challenge I face.

Zeroing In

And Jesus said to him,
What do you want Me to do for you?
MARK 10:51 AMPC

Stress can come upon us when we find ourselves running after a million different things, unable (or unwilling) to zero in on exactly what we want. When Jesus encountered a blind beggar calling out His name, He stopped and asked him, "What do you want me to do for you?" Although Jesus knew the man wanted sight, not alms, He made no move until the beggar said to Him: "Master, let me receive my sight" (verse 51 AMPC). "And Jesus said to him, Go your way; your faith has healed you. And at once he received his sight and accompanied Jesus on the road" (verse 52 AMPC).

Take some time now to stop and consider: What do you really want Jesus to do for you? Then pray and go your way, and your faith will heal you as you follow Jesus down the road.

Lord, help me to zero in on what I really want
then trust in You as I follow Your pathway.

Spinning Our Wheels

*I have strength for all things in Christ Who empowers
me [I am ready for anything and equal to anything
through Him Who infuses inner strength into me;
I am self-sufficient in Christ's sufficiency].*

PHILIPPIANS 4:13 AMPC

Oftentimes stress comes to us because we think we are strong enough to do it all, regardless of what our spiritual life and practice look like. But Jesus has clearly told us that unless we have a close and active relationship with Him, abiding in Him 24-7, we'll only be spinning our wheels. Because apart from Him, we can do nothing (see John 15:5).

Thus, we need to delve daily into the Word, believe God's promises, walk in His way, and pray, pray, pray. When we do, we realize we don't need to do it all. But for what He wants us to do, He'll give us all the strength we need.

*I know I am nothing without You, Lord. So I
come to You now for the strength to do what
You have called me to do. In Jesus' name, amen.*

The Remedy of Forgiveness

*Clothe yourselves with tenderhearted mercy, kindness,
humility, gentleness, and patience. Make allowance for
each other's faults, and forgive anyone who offends you.
Remember, the Lord forgave you, so you must forgive others.*
COLOSSIANS 3:12–13 NLT

It's amazing how well God knows His people, how much
His Word is a remedy for all our ills. God knows forgiveness
benefits us not only spiritually but physically as well. In fact,
forgiving others has been proven to lower not only stress but
depression—and blood pressure! It also improves cholesterol
levels and sleep! But it's not just saying the words "I forgive
you"; it's making a conscious decision to release all your
negative feelings toward that person and what he or she has
done—whether or not you believe the individual deserves
your forgiveness. Even if that person is yourself.

And the bonus to all this is that as you forgive others, God
forgives you! So go deep. Check in with yourself. Who do you
need to forgive?

*Lord, bring to my mind those I need to forgive,
and help me to do so in this moment.*

God's Goodness

*[What, what would have become of me] had I not believed
that I would see the Lord's goodness in the land of the living!
Wait and hope for and expect the Lord; be brave and of good
courage and let your heart be stout and enduring.*
PSALM 27:13–14 AMPC

When we feel as if the world is crashing down upon us, it can be difficult, if not impossible, to lift ourselves up. That's when we need to muster all the energy we have to ponder the words of Psalm 27:13–14 and then write them upon our hearts. For only God and His Word have the power to lift us up out of ourselves and into His light.

King David of the Bible, the author of these verses, knew that to keep his head above the fray, he had to have faith, to believe he would see God bring something good into his life—no matter how dire the situation. With courage and perseverance, he then waited in expectation of God's goodness.

*I know I'll see Your goodness in
this land and in my life, Lord!*

Trust

*Trust (lean on, rely on, and be confident) in the Lord
and do good; so shall you dwell in the land and feed
surely on His faithfulness, and truly you shall be fed.*
PSALM 37:3 AMPC

God wants you to trust in Him. To actually lean on Him, knowing
He alone can hold you up, give you the strength to stand. He
wants you to know you can rely on Him, confident that what
He has promised in His Word is a promise to you personally,
no holds barred. When you have that trust, you can then do
as He wishes. You can lead a life of stressing less, of following
in His steps, of doing His good. And when you are leading that
kind of life, believing in Him with your entire heart, all your
needs will be provided for.

Trust in God, the One who has loved you and provided for
you from the beginning, and all else will fall into place.

*Lord, I am counting on You, trusting You are holding me in
Your hand. Help me to rest secure in that knowledge.*

True Delight

*Delight yourself also in the Lord, and He will give
you the desires and secret petitions of your heart.*
PSALM 37:4 AMPC

It's easy to get stressed out, pulled in a thousand different ways as we try to fulfill our own desires or those of other people. In the quest to "satisfy" ourselves or others, our true path is obscured. Then when we actually obtain what we (or others) desire, we find that either it doesn't satisfy or another desire is just around the corner, and we begin the chase all over again.

God wants you to realize the only desire that can give you true rest and peace in this life is delighting yourself in Him, making closeness and fellowship with Him your only goal. Doing so not only will put all your other desires in their rightful place as your wants begin to line up with His, but it will give you rest from chasing the seemingly never-ending wants.

*Lord, I'm setting myself down, giving myself time to just rest
and take pleasure in You—my true delight and desire.*

Bringing Out the Best

Commit your way to the Lord [roll and repose each care of your load on Him]; trust (lean on, rely on, and be confident) also in Him and He will bring it to pass.
PSALM 37:5 AMPC

Turn everything in Your life over to God and trust that He will give you all the strength, wisdom, and help you need as you walk with Him. Let all the insults, problems, issues, comments, stresses roll right off your back and into His hands. He'll know what to do with them. Rest in the knowledge that you can trust God; He knows what He is doing, He sees the end, and all things will work out for good.

Have confidence in the One who was trusted by Abraham, whose son was saved by a ram. Rely on the One who was trusted by Joseph, a slave, then a prisoner, and finally a powerful ruler in Egypt.

*Lord, I'm committing my way to You,
knowing You will bring out the best in me.*

Quietness and Contentment

Be still and rest in the Lord; wait for Him and
patiently lean yourself upon Him; fret not
yourself because of him who prospers in his way.
PSALM 37:7 AMPC

As you begin to alleviate your stress by trusting and delighting yourself in the Lord, committing your way to Him, you will find yourself more still, more at peace, more able to rest in God. You will stop comparing your life to the lives of others who always seem to be one step ahead of you. Instead, you'll be patiently waiting for God, expecting and knowing He will do all good things in His time. You need not fear or fret. You and your life are in God's good hands, and this knowledge brings a wonderful new quiet and contentment into your life, a steadiness you've never experienced before.

Lord, here I am, leaning back upon You, listening to Your
breath as it aligns with mine. Fill me with peace beyond
understanding as I commit my path and desires to You,
trusting and delighting in You and Your love.

Do What You Can

"She did what she could when she could."
MARK 14:8 MSG

In Mark 14, a woman, her heart and spirit prompted by God, poured expensive perfume on Jesus' head. Witnesses muttered that she wasted perfume that could have been sold and the money given to the poor. But Jesus told them to leave her alone: "She did what she could when she could—she pre-anointed my body for burial. And you can be sure. . .what she just did is going to be talked about admiringly" (verses 8–9 MSG).

God wants you to be open to the Spirit and follow His promptings, to do what He would have you do, with what He gives you, when you can do it. And put the results, comments, consequences in His hands. Each day, listen, do, let what you didn't get done go, and then rest in Him, satisfied you have done what you could.

Lord, help me to do what I can and leave
the rest in Your amazingly capable hands.

First a Responder

When I am afraid, I put my trust in you. In God, whose word I praise, in God I trust; I shall not be afraid. . . . This I know, that God is for me. In God, whose word I praise, in the LORD, whose word I praise, in God I trust; I shall not be afraid.
PSALM 56:3–4, 9–11 ESV

David wrote the above words when he was in trouble. Three times he talks of his trust in God, how because of that trust, he need not fear anything or anyone. Three times he says he praises God's Word, reminding himself of how God's promises have come true for him in the past. And amid all this trusting and praising, he writes eight power-filled words: "This I know, that God is for me."

Use these words to help you be a responder instead of a reactor when stressful situations arise.

I need not fear because I know You are for me, God. I praise You and the power of Your Word!

Awake Rejoicing

This is the day that the Lord has made;
let us rejoice and be glad in it.
PSALM 118:24 ESV

Dale Evans Rogers said, "Every day we live is a priceless gift of God, loaded with possibilities to learn something new, to gain fresh insights." How wonder-filled would our day be if we awoke rejoicing because of the new day the Lord has made for us?

Why not deter stress by memorizing the words of Psalm 118:24 and saying them aloud before your feet hit the floor each day? Be curious about what you might learn that day, what God-incidence (i.e., a spiritual coincidence) might occur. Keep your eyes open for God's hand in all circumstances. And praise Him for the beauty of the ordinary, everyday people and things that surround you. Let your joy transform your face into a smile as you experience the priceless gift of life.

I'm rejoicing in the precious moments You have given
me today, Lord, and keeping my eyes open for You!

The Tower of Power

The name of the Lord is a strong tower; the [consistently] righteous man [upright and in right standing with God] runs into it and is safe, high [above evil] and strong.
PROVERBS 18:10 AMPC

Some days there is nowhere to go but up. It's a fact. Not all moments in our day are going to be rosy. But thankfully God has provided an exit plan for just such harrowing, stress-filled moments. When the going gets tough, get going to God. Shout His name and head for His presence. Run, climb, escape to Him—mentally, spiritually, emotionally, even physically if a church or chapel is nearby—a place of safety and strength, high above anything you are going through. With His presence surrounding you, nothing can really harm you. And you are given a space to catch your breath, calm your spirit, quiet your mind, settle your soul. Stay as long as you'd like until you're ready to face the challenge before you.

I'm running to You, Lord, my Tower of Power. For in You, I know I'm safe.

Weighed Down

Cast your burden on the Lord [releasing the weight of it] and He will sustain you; He will never allow the [consistently] righteous to be moved (made to slip, fall, or fail).
PSALM 55:22 AMPC

Proverbs 12:25 (AMPC) says, "Anxiety in a man's heart weighs it down." So what are we to do with our worries and stresses that have become so burdensome we are stooped low and feel we can no longer breathe? God wants us to come to Him every day—or every moment of every day, if needed—and leave all that weight on our hearts in His hands. When we do, He may not remove us from whatever situation we find ourselves in, but He'll keep us strong and give us peace in the midst of it. And once our hearts, minds, and souls are no longer burdened, God will make sure no one and nothing will push us off the course He's set for our lives.

What anxiety is weighing you down? Give it to God; then stand tall.

Lord, show me what burdens I need to give You.

Out of the Depths

*He [God] gives wisdom to the wise and knowledge
to those who have understanding! He reveals the
deep and secret things; He knows what is in the
darkness, and the light dwells with Him!*
DANIEL 2:21–22 AMPC

When you don't know what to do, when you are searching for an answer, when you are stressing for a blessing, go to God's Word. See it as "the Word of God which speaks out of the depths of an almost unimaginable past into the depths of ourselves" (Frederick Buechner, *Listening to Your Life,* June 14 reading).

Within God's story lies your own. Pray that He will give you the wisdom and knowledge you need to rise above your distress. Look for the secret He is aching to impart. Let Him show you the path to His light. Determine to allow His deep to call to your deep (see Psalm 42:7).

*God, speak out of Your depths and into mine.
Reveal in Your Word what You would have me know.*

God's Draw

In my distress I cried out to the LORD; yes, I prayed to my God for help. He heard me from his sanctuary; my cry to him reached his ears. . . . He reached down from heaven and rescued me; he drew me out of deep waters.
PSALM 18:6, 16 NLT

In times when you don't know what to do, where to go, turn to God in prayer. Imagine God's right hand reaching out to save you. Know that He will give you whatever strength and encouragement you need to continue on. He will protect you from all that's coming against you.

Never doubt that God has a plan for your life and is working it out—even this very moment. You opened this book to this page and are reading these words for a reason. For reassurance that God is still speaking into your life with a love beyond comprehension.

Lord, I rest in the knowledge that You will see me through all things, that You will give me the strength I need to live the life You've planned for me.

Arms Wide Open

Carefully build yourselves up in this most holy faith by
praying in the Holy Spirit, staying right at the center
of God's love, keeping your arms open and outstretched,
ready for the mercy of our Master, Jesus Christ.
This is the unending life, the real life!
JUDE 1:20–21 MSG

Sometimes a woman prays an SOS prayer: "God, help me!"
Sometimes she prays out of habit, using words so rehearsed or
so-long memorized that their meaning is obscured, unrealized,
forgotten. Then there are prayers that are based not on God's
will but on her own agenda, wants, desires, needs.

To build up her faith, a woman is advised to pray in the
Holy Spirit. That means praying in rhythm with the Spirit, in
agreement with His will. That's how she will stay at the center
of God's love with arms wide open, ready to receive all Jesus
has to offer.

Help me, Holy Spirit, to be in harmony with
Your will, Your agenda, Your plans, not mine.
Keep me at the center of God's love.

Calling God

"This is God's Message, the God who made earth, made it livable and lasting, known everywhere as GOD: *'Call to me and I will answer you. I'll tell you marvelous and wondrous things that you could never figure out on your own.' "*
JEREMIAH 33:3 MSG

You never know when God is going to reveal something to you, some truth you need to know, some secret to help you connect the dots, see His hand, discover the solution, find some hope. And God can deliver that message no matter where you are! (Jeremiah received the words of this verse while he was locked up in jail!) But you have to call on God. You have to pray to Him. When you do, He'll answer you, telling you things you otherwise would never know! He—the Creator of the universe, the One who knows how everything works—will help you figure things out.

The formula is simple: Call. Pray. Listen. Then marvel at the wonder of the knowledge of God.

Dear Lord, here I am! Speak!
Tell me what You'd have me know.

Get Going

GOD addressed Samuel: "So, how long are you going to mope over Saul? You know I've rejected him as king over Israel. Fill your flask with anointing oil and get going. I'm sending you to Jesse of Bethlehem. I've spotted the very king I want among his sons."

1 SAMUEL 16:1 MSG

You had a plan. But things didn't turn out the way you thought they would. Yet you still seem to be sulking, brooding over what seems to be a lost opportunity, mourning what could've been, maybe even trying to force things to work out right.

God wants you to stop stressing over what could've been. He's ready for you to move on, to get going, to take the next step in His plan.

Ask God what His next move for you is. He has already spotted your next opportunity to cooperate with His plan and work out His good for all concerned. So what are you waiting for? Get going.

I'm not sure, Lord, why things didn't work out, but I know You have a plan. So I'm ready, Lord. Where to?

God in Action

"When two of you get together on anything at all on earth
and make a prayer of it, my Father in heaven goes into action.
And when two or three of you are together because of me,
you can be sure that I'll be there."
MATTHEW 18:20 MSG

Author Emily Kimbrough said, "Remember, we all stumble, every one of us. That's why it's a comfort to go hand in hand." God takes this further in Ecclesiastes 4:12 (MSG) by telling us, "By yourself you're unprotected. With a friend you can face the worst. Can you round up a third? A three-stranded rope isn't easily snapped."

Jesus makes this idea even more powerful. He says when two pray, our Father God "goes into action"! And when believers are together in Jesus' name, we can be certain He's right in the thick of things!

So stress less by grabbing a believer (or two) by the hand. Tap into the comfort and strength a duo or threesome provides. Expect Jesus to join you. And watch God go into action!

Here we are, Lord! We're tapping into You!

Patient Faith

But God remembered Noah and all the beasts and all the
livestock that were with him in the ark. And God made
a wind blow over the earth, and the waters subsided.
GENESIS 8:1 ESV

Thinking that God has forgotten you? That He has left you adrift in a stress storm lasting forty days and nights? Don't believe those lies for a minute. God remembers you.

Just when you think the waters of chaos couldn't get any higher, God will stop the flood. As the waters begin to recede, He'll set you to rest on dry land. And as the waters continue to abate, God will renew the world around you, preparing the ground for your next step upon dry land.

Be patient. For Noah, 370 days passed between the first drop of rain and the moment Noah and company left the ark. Have faith. For it was by and because of faith that Noah followed God, built an ark, saved his family, and had the opportunity to become "intimate with God" (Hebrews 11:7 MSG).

I'm trusting in Your timing, Lord. Bless my faith.

Celebrating the Spiritual Woman

Therefore we do not become discouraged (utterly spiritless, exhausted, and wearied out through fear). Though our outer man is [progressively] decaying and wasting away, yet our inner self is being [progressively] renewed day after day.
2 CORINTHIANS 4:16 AMPC

Yes, our bodies are changing day by day. From the minute we are born, our earth suits begin to wear out. That's the not-so-good news. The better news is that no matter what's happening to our outer woman (physical self), the inner woman (spiritual self) is being refreshed, renewed, day after day! That's because "we consider and look not to the things that are seen but to the things that are unseen; for the things that are visible are temporal (brief and fleeting), but the things that are invisible are deathless and everlasting" (2 Corinthians 4:18 AMPC).

So, keeping your eyes on Christ, stop stressing over the new laugh lines, and instead celebrate the beauty of your inner spirit.

Lord, I don't want to be focused on the material girl but rather celebrate the spiritual woman! Help me to keep my eyes on the unseen.

Take Confidence

"With him is an arm of flesh, but with us is the LORD our God, to help us and to fight our battles." And the people took confidence from the words of Hezekiah king of Judah.
2 CHRONICLES 32:8 ESV

Much of stress comes from lack of confidence in our abilities, lack of faith that God can help us do all He's called us to do.

But the truth is that because God is in our lives, He's empowering and equipping us to do all He wants us to do—no matter how big or small the job! And God is not just an arm of flesh, a sometimes-there human helper. He's the Lord of the universe, the Master Planner, the One who can make the sun stop in the sky! Take confidence from those facts! Know that He's helping you fight every battle you encounter. As He does, others who see it will know that "this work [was] accomplished with the help of our God" (Nehemiah 6:16 ESV).

Grow my confidence in You, Lord!

Out of Line

If we live by the [Holy] Spirit, let us also walk by the Spirit. [If by the Holy Spirit we have our life in God, let us go forward walking in line, our conduct controlled by the Spirit.]
GALATIANS 5:25 AMPC

When stress begins to rule our lives, the root cause is apt to be that we are following the world instead of the Word, in step with society instead of the Spirit. Stress is a signal that we are to stop, look up from the path our feet are on, and take stock of where we are standing. Then we must choose to get back on track, back in line with what we profess as Christians, asking God to recalculate our route, to change the vision we have before us, from ours to His, before we stumble even further away from what He would have us be and do.

Lord, I have stepped out of line with the Spirit.
Help me to get back on His path. Show me the way I should go. Change my thoughts to be more like Yours.

Everything We Need

We're depending on God; he's everything we need.
What's more, our hearts brim with joy since we've taken
for our own his holy name. Love us, God, with all
you've got—that's what we're depending on.
PSALM 33:20–21 MSG

There's no reason to stress when we realize that God is everything we need. He is our help, our shield, our fortress. When we are abiding in Him, we are filled with the joy His presence brings.

Other humans will let us down. That's a given. But God won't. We can depend on Him through thick and thin. He constantly has His eye upon us, watching, waiting to step in and save us when we get stuck. He keeps us together—heart, body, soul, mind, and spirit.

Lean your entire self upon Him, and soon your stress will disappear in the power of His love and light.

I'm depending on You, Lord, for all I need. You've
brought me out of the depths of despair so many
times before. Do so again as I lean back on You.

First Necessity

*If you seek Him [inquiring for and of Him, craving Him
as your soul's first necessity], He will be found by you.*
2 Chronicles 15:2 AMPC

The Spirit of God came on Azariah and he spoke to King Asa.
He told him how in times past, "there was no peace to him
who went out nor to him who came in, but great and vexing
afflictions and disturbances were upon all the inhabitants"
(verse 5 AMPC). (Sound familiar?) But if he, and they, went
seeking God, they would find Him. "Be strong, therefore,"
said Azariah, "and let not your hands be weak and slack, for
your work shall be rewarded" (verse 7 AMPC).

When you have nothing but trouble, when stress is weighing
you down, immobilizing you from doing anything for God,
seek Him. You'll find Him waiting to hear your voice and to
give you peace of mind, body, spirit, and soul.

*Lord, I come seeking Your face, craving Your presence
above all else. Give me the peace only You can give.
Then strengthen my hands to do Your will.*

From Groan to Good

*The Holy Spirit helps us in our weakness. For example, we
don't know what God wants us to pray for. But the Holy Spirit
prays for us with groanings that cannot be expressed in words.*
ROMANS 8:26 NLT

Amid a stressful situation or a crisis, our emotions threaten to
take over. Thoughts scatter. Hearts thump out of control. We
cannot find our voices or even utter a sane word. That's when
God's Spirit steps in and rescues us.

In these moments, we don't have the strength or calm to
zero in on what God wants us to pray for. But it doesn't matter.
All we need to do is moan and groan, and we trigger the Holy
Spirit who prays for us! And God, who knows our hearts, will
"get" it. He'll "get" us. He'll examine our situation and work
out whatever's happening for good.

*Sometimes I feel so helpless, Spirit, so wordless. But You
know me. You see me. Be my Comforter, my Messenger.
Tell God all about it. Turn my groan into something good.*

God's a Keeper

I, the Lord, am its Keeper; I water it every moment;
lest anyone harm it, I guard and keep it night and day.
Isaiah 27:3 AMPC

You're someone the Lord has planted in this time, in this place, in this world. And your Father God has promised to tend you, to water you with love, compassion, mercy, forgiveness, and grace. He'll send His angels to guard and protect you while you're awake and when you sleep. There's nothing He won't do to keep you safe and close to Him. That's His part to play. Yours is to keep yourself close to Him.

To do that, immerse yourself in His Word, breathe in His presence, seek His face, and speak to Him through prayer. Be the flower He has created you to be, the lily that has no worries for she knows her gardener is in her midst. And when you do, you will find yourself not stressed but blooming where you are planted.

Lord, You're my Keeper, constantly tending to me,
protecting me. Help me to bloom where
You've planted me—for Your glory!

You Choose

*"Today I am giving you a choice between life and death,
between prosperity and disaster. For I command you this
day to love the Lord your God and to keep his commands,
decrees, and regulations by walking in his ways."*
DEUTERONOMY 30:15–16 NLT

Each day God gives you a choice between life with less stress
or deathlike life with more stress. To have the former, simply
love God, do as He commands, and walk on the path He has
set before you. "If you do this, you will live and multiply, and
the Lord your God will bless you and the land you are about to
enter and occupy" (verse 16 NLT). But if you choose the latter,
if you decide to serve other, lesser gods (such as money, pride,
greed, envy, etc.), you will find a much harder road ahead and
a zombielike existence.

God has given His people the freedom and the power of
choice. What will you choose? Whom will you serve?

*Lord, thank You for the power of choice.
I choose to serve You today!*

Turning

Before him [Josiah] there was no king like him,
who turned to the LORD with all his heart and with
all his soul and with all his might, according to all the
Law of Moses, nor did any like him arise after him.
2 KINGS 23:25 ESV

It's easy to get caught up in the world's wants, the media mayhem, the technology torrent, the society schism, but God wants you less stressed, turned to Him with all your heart, soul, and strength.

So today endeavor to turn away from the chaos and crisis surrounding you and lean into God. For as you "turn your eyes upon Jesus" and "look full in His wonderful face," you'll find "the things of earth will grow strangely dim, in the light of His glory and grace" (lyrics to "Turn Your Eyes upon Jesus" by Helen H. Lemmel [1922]).

Lord, when I turn to You with all I am, my stress fades away.
So I look to You now, Lord. Catch me up in You.

Take Your Stand

During the night an angel of God opened the jailhouse door and led them out. He said, "Go to the Temple and take your stand. Tell the people. . .about this Life." Promptly obedient, they entered the Temple at daybreak and went on with their teaching.
ACTS 5:19–20 MSG

In the same way God's angel rescued the apostles—even while men stood guard—God can rescue you from whatever has you imprisoned. Yet He doesn't help you escape so you can spend more time watching TV. He wants you to be obedient to what He would have you do.

God has given you life for a reason. He has a calling for you. Once you have made Jesus Lord of your life, it's time to be free, to be brave, to have peace in Him, and to be obedient to His voice. He wants you to take your stand and share His life with others.

Lord, break my soul out of its imprisonment. Help me to rise above my stress so I can make the wonders of Your way and life known to others, freeing them for You.

On Purpose

O God. . . I will hide beneath the shadow of your wings
until the danger passes by. I cry out to God Most High. . .
who will fulfill his purpose for me. He will send
help from heaven to rescue me.
PSALM 57:1–3 NLT

When we're on the run, feeling as if troubles are chasing us down, there's only one place to go. To God, the One we trust with all our being. When the storms, the hawk, or the wolf is on our tail, we can be as chicks who scramble to hunker down under the wings of their mother hen, confident she will keep them whole, warm, and dry. We're confident God won't let us down, that He will send help from heaven to pluck us out of trouble, because He has a plan, a purpose for our life.

When stress prowls around your door, run to God. Hide in Him until the storm passes. Then live your purpose—on purpose.

Here I come, Lord, taking refuge beneath Your wings
until I have the courage to walk Your way once again.

As High as the Heavens

My heart is confident in you, O God. . . . No wonder I can sing
your praises! Wake up, my heart! Wake up, O lyre and harp!
I will wake the dawn with my song. . . . I will sing your praises.
. . . For your unfailing love is as high as the heavens.
PSALM 57:7–10 NLT

A great way to beat stress is to fall asleep with an uplifting,
confidence-supplying Bible verse in your mind. A verse that gives
your heart strength and peace, allowing not only for a restful
night but also a joyful morning. Wouldn't it be wonderful to
be singing praises to God upon waking rather than rehearsing
problems in your mind?

Try claiming a life-giving promise or truth about God or His
love and faithfulness before you close your eyes. And discover
how much your stress lessens and your praises increase, reaching
"as high as the heavens."

Lord, give me a verse to fall asleep to, one that,
with the morning light, will help my heart take flight.

Not Stressed but Blessed

And blessed (happy, to be envied) is she who believed
that there would be a fulfillment of the things
that were spoken to her from the Lord.
LUKE 1:45 AMPC

How blessed was Mary because she believed God could do the impossible—for her and her cousin Elizabeth. Mary believed the angel Gabriel when he told her she had nothing to fear (see verse 30). That she would become pregnant without having slept with a man and that her son Jesus would be God's Son (see verses 34–35). That her aged cousin Elizabeth would become pregnant in her old age (see verse 36). That nothing was impossible with God (see verse 37).

Happy will you be if you believe God's promises to you and submit to Him, loving Him and serving Him, as Mary did.

I am Your servant, Lord, and I believe You will make Your
promises come true in my life. Because of these two things,
I am not stressed but blessed! May everything You have
said come true. For everything is possible with You!

Blessings Abound

"I belong to the Lord, body and soul," replied Mary,
"let it happen as you say." And at this the angel left her.
LUKE 1:38 PHILLIPS

How readily do you submit to the Lord, give Him ownership over you? How much you submit to God directly correlates to how much you truly trust Him—to do what He says He will do in His Word, to stick to His promises, to work out all things for your good, to overcome the darkness that seems determined to surround you, and to lead you into the light.

Build up your trust in God by keeping track of answered prayers, by recounting your blessings before bed, and by memorizing and expecting His promises as recorded in the Bible. For when you give all of yourself to God, when you let go and let God, blessings begin to abound.

Help me, Lord, to give up all of myself and my life
to You so that I can fully become Your obedient
daughter, confident in and blessed by You.

Four Ways

*Delight yourselves in God, yes, find your joy in
him at all times. Have a reputation for gentleness,
and never forget the nearness of your Lord.*
PHILIPPIANS 4:4–5 PHILLIPS

This scripture covers at least four ways to keep stress at bay.
The first is to delight yourself in God. Revel in His Word. Take
pleasure just being in His company. The second is to find your
joy in the Lord at all times! Look for Him hiding around the
corner. Laugh when He works things out beyond anything you
could have imagined. See Him in the smile of a stranger. The
third is to be known for your gentleness. People admire the
soft-spoken, those who exhibit contentment no matter what
is happening in their lives. And the last is to "never forget the
nearness of your Lord." Knowing He is right beside you, loving
you, protecting you, delighting in you, is a wonderful thing to
keep in the forefront of your mind, just as He keeps you in the
forefront of His.

*Lord, thank You for bringing such
joy and delight into my life!*

Learn to Be Content

I have learned to be content, whatever the circumstances may be. I know now how to live when things are difficult and I know how to live when things are prosperous. In general and in particular I have learned the secret of facing either poverty or plenty.
PHILIPPIANS 4:11–12 PHILLIPS

How simple it was for us to be content when we were younger. Our tears, if any, lasted only until we got our crayon back, were eating our favorite cookie, saw our mother's smile, or heard our father's laugh. It was those simple things that made us happy.

Why not have that attitude now? Practice finding joy and contentment in the simple things life gives you—a sunset, a fallen leaf, a flower petal, a smile from a loved one, a good book, a soft song, a call from a friend. . . The list could go on and on.

Learn to be content and your stress will have no place to hang its hat.

Help me, Lord, to find contentment in the little things—all of which are Your miracles.

The Right Spirit

We can be full of joy here and now even in our trials and troubles. Taken in the right spirit these very things will give us patient endurance; this in turn will develop a mature character, and a character of this sort produces a steady hope, a hope that will never disappoint us.
ROMANS 5:3–4 PHILLIPS

Being joyful is a matter of choice. It depends on how we choose to respond to the things that come our way. With the right spirit, we'll find a way to patiently endure. Having the right spirit will help us to grow up into God and develop a character marked by a steady hope.

What's happening in your life right now? What's your attitude toward it? Are you looking for the blessing—no matter how small—amid the trouble?

If you feel stuck in your current attitude or perspective, take a moment each night to write down five good things happening in your life, and watch how that practice will revive your spirit.

Lord, help me to have the right spirit—
no matter what's happening in my life!

Celebrate Together

"The master was full of praise. 'Well done, my good and faithful servant. You have been faithful in handling this small amount, so now I will give you many more responsibilities. Let's celebrate together!' "
MATTHEW 25:21 NLT

When you've accomplished something good, no matter how big or little, take time to celebrate. Look up to God, thanking Him for His help. Know that He will be full of praise for you. He will be giving you an "atta girl" for a job well done. For in all you do, you aren't really serving other people but Him, your Master!

As you continue to handle the little things well, God will give you more things to do. But the main point here is to take time to celebrate with God. Pause in His presence and pleasure. Know He is watching you, that He approves of you and sees you as faithful and praiseworthy. Then praise Him back!

I'm so excited to celebrate with You today, Lord! What shall we tackle together next?

Lighten Up

But he's already made it plain how to live, what to do, what God is looking for in. . .women. It's quite simple: Do what is fair and just to your neighbor, be compassionate and loyal in your love, and don't take yourself too seriously—take God seriously.

MICAH 6:8 MSG

One of the best ways to de-stress is to get out of your own head by doing something for someone else. You may think that you don't have the time or energy to help a neighbor, babysit the child of a harassed mom, or visit an elderly woman in her retirement home. Or maybe you think you're already doing so much for everyone else in your life, you can't possibly carve out five more minutes to serve anyone else.

But when you do something for someone else outside of your usual routine, the benefits far outweigh any time or effort you expend. God is looking for you to lighten up about your own life and invest yourself in Him.

Help me to get out of my own head today, Lord.
Show me who to love.

Rock Out

Speak out to one another in psalms and hymns and
spiritual songs, offering praise with voices [and instruments]
and making melody with all your heart to the Lord,
at all times and for everything giving thanks in the name
of our Lord Jesus Christ to God the Father.
EPHESIANS 5:19–20 AMPC

Another way to de-stress by getting out of your own head is to exchange your mental machinations for God's. You can do that by singing praises to Him. Make melody with all you are, your mind, body, heart, and soul—no matter how off-key you might be! Singing God's praises and giving Him thanks for all the blessings He has bestowed upon you will lift your entire being, drawing you closer to the place He would have you be. You'll not only be uplifted but also gain all the strength and energy you need to continue on.

So what are you waiting for? Find a praise tune and rock out—for the Rock!

Lord, thank You so much for all You've done for me.
I lift my eyes and praise to You.

Mighty Power

Now all glory to God, who is able, through his
mighty power at work within us, to accomplish
infinitely more than we might ask or think.
EPHESIANS 3:20 NLT

Imagine it. God working so deeply within you. His creative power giving you the strength, the determination, the skill, the resources, the energy to do everything He has purposed you to do! And the means and ways to do it far beyond what you ever thought you could accomplish in your wildest dreams and imagination. He has given you power to do things you haven't even dared ask!

God has planted you in this world to do something marvelous and works through you to finish that job. You have all you need. So don't stress. Realize how blessed and power-filled you are as you live your life for His will and glory!

I am amazed, Lord, at how much You have equipped me
to do what You would have me do. Thank You for Your
mighty power working through me to bring You glory!

According to Your Need

This is what the Lord has commanded: Let every man gather of it as much as he will need. . . . When they measured it. . . he who gathered much had nothing over, and he who gathered little had no lack; each gathered according to his need.
EXODUS 16:16, 18 AMPC

God knows exactly what you need. He has promised to provide it. Your job is to trust He will do so. For when you begin to doubt that the One who created you and everything around you is going to be there for you, stress and anxiety quickly set in. You begin trying to provide everything you need all by yourself, leaving God out of the equation entirely. So stop. Take stock of what you've taken on, how much you're straining to gather "just in case." Bring the Great Provider back into the equation. Know that with the Good Shepherd first in your life, you can relax and say:

"The Lord is my Shepherd [to feed, guide, and shield me], I shall not lack" [Psalm 23:1 AMPC].

Ultimate Stain Remover

*For his unfailing love toward those who fear him is as great
as the height of the heavens above the earth. He has removed
our sins as far from us as the east is from the west.*
PSALM 103:11–12 NLT

God's unfathomable amount of love for you is the one constant
in your life. Although at times you may not understand why
certain things happen, you can always rest assured God will
never leave or forsake you. Because you recognize Him as the
Master and Creator and worship Him first in your life, you can
be assured of the greatness of His love for you. In fact, His love is
so huge that He has forgiven and forgotten every mistake you've
made, every offense you've committed. He has removed them
from you as far as "the east is from the west." That's a forever
thing, an eternal promise.

So stress no longer over past misdeeds. God has already
forgotten them. Instead, rest in Him, knowing you're forever
loved and forgiven.

*You, Lord, are the ultimate Stain Remover.
Thank You for loving me so much.*

Bearing Up

*I have loved you with an everlasting love; therefore
with loving-kindness have I drawn you and continued
My faithfulness to you. Again I will build you and
you will be built. . . ! You will again. . .go forth in
the dancing [chorus] of those who make merry.*
JEREMIAH 31:3–4 AMPC

Nothing can shake you up more than a situation—a word, a look, a loss—you didn't see coming, prompting you to react automatically by fight, flight, or freeze. Those are the times when any other little annoyance or problem added to that unexpected event makes the stress almost unbearable.

The key is to remember God loves you. He has called you, drawn you to Him so He can help you. He has given you promises to rise up on, words to stand on, hope to heal. This too shall pass. And, though it may not seem possible now, day by day the pain will abate until you find joy in life and in the Lord once again.

*Lord, help me to bear up. Be faithful in carrying
me as I faithfully put my hope in You.*

Recall, Recount, Pronounce

The Lord, the God of heaven, Who took me. . .from the
land of my family and my birth, Who spoke to me and
swore to me, saying, To your offspring I will give this
land—He will send His Angel before you, and you
will take a wife from there for my son.
GENESIS 24:7 AMPC

The clock was ticking. Time was of the essence when an old
Abraham, showing great trust in God, sent his servant to
find a wife for his son Isaac. Abraham recalled how God had
led him away from home to a foreign land of His choosing.
He recounted the promise God had made, saying this land
would be his children's. And now Abraham pronounces his
belief that God will send His angel before his servant as he
embarks upon this wife-seeking journey.

To become as trusting as Abraham, recall how God has led
you. Recount the promises He has made to you. Pronounce your
belief that God is sending His angels ahead of you.

Lead me on, Lord. Though I
know not where, I trust in You.

Request Success

*So humble yourselves under the mighty power of God,
and at the right time he will lift you up in honor. Give all
your worries and cares to God, for he cares about you.*

1 PETER 5:6–7 NLT

Abraham's servant sets off on his master's mission. After arriving at his destination, he stops and prays for guidance, saying, "O LORD, God of my master, Abraham. . . Please give me success today, and show unfailing love to my master, Abraham. See, I am standing here beside this spring, and the young women of the town are coming out to draw water. This is my request" (Genesis 24:12–14 NLT).

Instead of stressing out, allowing what-ifs to clamor around in his head, this dedicated and trustworthy servant stopped and prayed for guidance, outlining his and his master's situations and asking for success—and got it!

Stop. Pray for guidance. Present your situation to the Lord. Ask Him for success. And rise with peace, knowing your life is in good hands.

*Lord of lords, here's my request. . . .
Please grant me success!*

Ready, Willing, and Able

"So today when I came to the spring, I prayed. . . .
Before I had finished praying in my heart, I saw Rebekah."
GENESIS 24:42, 45 NLT

Before Abraham's servant had even finished praying his prayer, God answered it in the form of Rebekah, who then became Isaac's wife! As soon as the servant realized Rebekah fit all of Abraham's requirements for his son Isaac, "the man bowed low and worshiped the LORD" (verse 26).

God is ready, willing, and able to answer your prayers the same way. He has given you the promise, "I will answer them before they even call to me. While they are still talking about their needs, I will go ahead and answer their prayers!" (Isaiah 65:24 NLT). And once your prayers are answered, respond like Abraham's humble servant. Bow and worship your good Lord.

Lord, You amaze me. You answer my prayers before I
even approach You. Yet You still want me to say the words,
to pray from my heart. So here I am, Lord. I pray. . .

Persistence

But David persisted.
1 Samuel 17:34 NLT

Sometimes we find ourselves stressing out because we believe we're not doing what God has called us to do. In effect, we're just spinning our wheels, leading the lives others expect us to lead.

Before becoming king, David went to visit his brothers, found out about the taunts of Goliath, and figured he'd fight the giant no one else was willing to face. His brother got angry and told him to go back to tending sheep. But David stayed. Later King Saul told him, "You can't fight this giant. You're just a kid with no battle experience."

"But David persisted," claiming he'd already killed bears and lions to protect his father's sheep and goats, saying, "The Lord who rescued me from the claws of the lion and the bear will rescue me from this Philistine!" (1 Samuel 17:37 NLT).

Consider the naysayers and discouragers in your own life. Consider what God has been training you for. Then ask. . .

Lord, what's Your dream for my life?
What calling would You have me persist in?

Equipment

*He picked up five smooth stones from a stream and
put them into his shepherd's bag. Then, armed
only with his shepherd's staff and sling, he started
across the valley to fight the Philistine.*
1 SAMUEL 17:40 NLT

Once Saul was convinced David might have a chance against
the giant, he determined to outfit David, putting his own armor
on the boy. But once the gear was on, David could barely walk.
So he told Saul, "I can't go in these. . . . I'm not used to them"
(verse 39 NLT), and took the equipment off. David then went
off to face Goliath, equipped with a few stones, his staff, and
a sling, fully assured he would succeed in the power of God.

God has made you special, equipping you with simple tools
that fit you personally and giving you the confidence that you'll
succeed in His power.

*Help me de-stress, Lord, by exchanging this equipment
that doesn't fit me for the special gear You've fashioned
just for me to meet my challenges, enabling me to
succeed in Your power, not my own.*

Timing

He waited seven days, the time appointed by Samuel. But Samuel did not come to Gilgal, and the people were scattering from him. So Saul. . . offered the burnt offering. As soon as he had finished offering the burnt offering, behold, Samuel came.
1 SAMUEL 13:8–10 ESV

The prophet Samuel had told Saul to wait for him in Gilgal. When Samuel got there, he would make a sacrifice and tell Saul God's will for him. But Saul, reacting to the fear of the troops who were with him, decided to take matters into his own hands. The result of his bowing to circumstances instead of being obedient to and trusting God was that Saul's kingdom would cease and the Lord would assign a "man after his own heart" (verse 14 ESV) to rule His people.

God has His own particular timing for every event in your life. So don't stress. Be a woman after God's own heart. And may your prayer be this:

"I wait for the LORD, my soul waits, and in his word I hope" [Psalm 130:5 ESV].

Time and Place

The Lord gave this message to Jonah son of Amittai: "Get up and go to the great city of Nineveh." . . . But Jonah got up and went in the opposite direction to get away from the Lord. . . . Then Jonah prayed to the Lord his God from inside the fish.
Jonah 1:1–3; 2:1 NLT

Being in the wrong place at the wrong time can cause major stress. Jonah found that out when God told him to go one way and he headed in the opposite direction. Not only did the prophet end up on a ship during a terrible storm, but he ultimately landed in the belly of a whale. It was only after that whale vomited him back onto the shore that Jonah headed in God's direction.

Which way do you head when God asks you to "get up and go"?

Lord, You know where I am in my life. Show me the next steps. Lead me where You want me to go so that I'm walking in Your will and Your way.

The Right Equipment, Time, and Place

*"If you keep silent at this time, relief and deliverance will rise
for the Jews from another place. . . . And who knows whether
you have not come to the kingdom for such a time as this?"*
ESTHER 4:14 ESV

Esther had the right equipment to land her in the king's harem.
And she was in exactly the right place when a major threat arose
against God's people. Although she found herself caught amid
the machinations of men, her cousin gave her some sage advice,
telling her that perhaps she was in this time and place for a
reason. That God would work through her to deliver His people.

Queen Esther rose above the stressful situation by remaining
faithful. She ordered a fast to help ensure success then put
herself and the situation in God's hands, knowing the results
would be according to His will.

*You've equipped me, Lord, for a purpose.
Show me what You would have me do in this
time and place. I leave it all in Your hands.*

Powerful Word

God means what he says. What he says goes. His powerful
Word is sharp as a surgeon's scalpel, cutting through everything,
whether doubt or defense, laying us open to listen and obey.
HEBREWS 4:12 MSG

Stressed or distressed? Say a heartfelt prayer then dive deep into God's Word. It's alive and powerful, "making it active, operative, energizing, and effective" (Hebrews 4:12 AMPC). It'll go deep within, revealing what needs to be revealed. It'll give you guidance, wisdom, strength, knowledge. It'll pull you out of your present state, nurture and heal you where you need it the most. It'll give you a rock to stand on and the faith and courage to lean on God, trusting Him to carry you when you can no longer walk.

Find a verse that speaks to your heart. Then pray those words back to the Author, the Mighty One who dwells within you and invites you to shelter in His embrace.

Nothing is more powerful than Your Word, Lord. Tell me what
I need to hear, then listen as I whisper those words back to You.

Draw Near to God

Without faith it is impossible to please and be satisfactory to Him. For whoever would come near to God must [necessarily] believe that God exists and that He is the rewarder of those who earnestly and diligently seek Him [out].
HEBREWS 11:6 AMPC

The nearer you draw to God, the further you move away from stress. It's a fact. But when you draw near, you have to believe that God exists and that He will reward your faith by staying true to His promises.

Go deeper. Read about the heroes of faith in Hebrews 11. There you will discover how faith "prompted" Noah, Abraham, Jacob, Moses, and Rahab (verses 7, 9, 21, 23, 31). It "urged on" Abraham (verse 8), gave Isaac visionary "eyes" (verse 20), and gave Sarah "physical power" (verse 11). It "actuated" Joseph (verse 22) and "aroused" and "motivated" Moses (verses 24, 27). (See AMPC.)

Faith is living and active. Draw near to God, the ultimate Promise Keeper and Faith Maker.

Lord, I'm coming close, relying on Your promises. Move me with faith—prompt me, urge me on, inspire me to live for You.

Rising Up

Those who wait for the Lord [who expect, look for, and hope in Him] shall change and renew their strength and power; they shall lift their wings and mount up [close to God] as eagles [mount up to the sun]; they shall run and not be weary, they shall walk and not faint or become tired.
ISAIAH 40:31 AMPC

When stress seems to have gotten the best of you, the words of Isaiah 40:31 will help you pull your eyes off yourself and lift them to the Lord. So look up. Know God is on your side. Be patiently expectant, knowing He will come through for you. He already has a plan. In fact, He's working things out behind the scenes. He will fill you with strength and power to meet the challenges and opportunities in front of you.

So open up your wings. Take a deep breath and see yourself rising up to Him, as close as you can get. Feel the stress fall away as you head for the Son.

I'm rising up to You, Lord.

Pray, Then Pry

Behold, I stand at the door and knock;
if anyone hears and listens to and heeds My
voice and opens the door, I will come in to him.
REVELATION 3:20 AMPC

When you're in the midst of a stressful situation, getting yourself to sit down and pray may take some effort. But that's exactly what Jesus is waiting for you to do. He's standing there knocking, waiting for you to open the door to His presence. Once you do, He can then open up your heart to receive what He's telling you.

The Lord did that for Lydia. "One of those who listened to us was a woman named Lydia. . . . And the Lord opened her heart to pay attention to what was said" (Acts 16:14 AMPC). He's waiting right now to do the same for you.

Pray, then pry that door open. Let the Son's light in.

I know You're waiting, Lord. So here I am,
opening my door to You, so that You can open
the door to my heart. Speak to me, Lord.

Love Meets You

O my Strength, I will watch for you, for you, O God,
are my fortress. My God in his steadfast love will meet me.
PSALM 59:9–10 ESV

Stress comes, in part, from trying to do things in your own strength. But once you acknowledge that whatever strength you have comes from God, a weight lifts. For when you feel weak, you can turn your gaze away from your worries and up to God. Set yourself to watch for your true Strength. Hang out in His fortress, His high tower. Know that no matter what the problem, situation, or circumstance, the Lord, the Prince of Peace, the mighty Spirit, is there, loving you, holding you up, empowering you. In fact, He's been watching you. He's already gone ahead to pave the way before you. Wait. Watch. His love will meet you.

Here I am, Lord, waiting, watching, knowing You are the Prince to whom I can run, whose love meets me where I am.

No Limit

Thanks be to God, Who gives us the victory [making us conquerors] through our Lord Jesus Christ.
1 CORINTHIANS 15:57 AMPC

The moment you feel beaten down by stress is the exact right time to remember God has already given you victory as a believer in Christ. So what is there to fear, to worry about? The One who spoke the world into being is on your side. The One who parted the Red Sea, provided manna in the wilderness, saved Daniel in the lions' den, and appeared in the midst of a fiery furnace from which three of God's people emerged unscathed. There is no limit to His strength and wisdom.

Give thanks to God right now, realizing that in Him you are more than a conqueror in this world—and the next.

Lord, write upon the walls of my mind the fact that in You, I have all the strength I need to overcome because I share the power of the One You raised up and into the light.

Calling and Calming

*"Do not be afraid or discouraged. For the
LORD your God is with you wherever you go."*
JOSHUA 1:9 NLT

Stress thrives when we're distracted by the world instead of
focused on God's calling. Fortunately, God's Word helps us find
our way out, just as He helped Joshua, the man called to lead
God's people into the Promised Land. Three times, God tells
Joshua to be strong and courageous. Then He tells him to obey
God's Book of Instruction, meditating on it continually. For only
when we make God's Word part of ourselves will we succeed
in what God is calling us to do. As we hide His Word in our
hearts, He promises to be with us wherever we go, making the
task before us less intimidating.

Get refocused on your calling and in turn receive God's
calming by spending time reading, studying, and applying the
words of Joshua 1:6–9. Be strong and courageous. Live God's
Word. Apply it to your life. And know God is with you.

*I'm realigning my life with You, Lord. Help me
to find my way back to Your purpose for me.*

Staying Power

*Take the old prophets as your mentors. . . . What a gift
life is to those who stay the course! You've heard, of course,
of Job's staying power, and you know how God brought it all
together for him at the end. That's because God cares,
cares right down to the last detail.*

JAMES 5:11 MSG

In the short run, it may seem easy to wallow in stress, even to
brag about it sometimes, saying things like, "I'm so busy I don't
even have time to breathe." We seem to wear our busyness as
a strange badge of honor.

But God would have us do as the old prophets did, those
who "put up with anything, went through everything, and never
once quit, all the time honoring God" (James 5:11 MSG). Don't
let the world's woes get you down. Don't stress about what
might've been. Instead, "Be patient. . . . Stay steady and strong"
(James 5:7 MSG). God's got you. He'll take care of everything.

*Lord, help me to stay the course, loving and serving You,
knowing You're taking care of everything.*

Heart Check

"Our fathers refused to obey him, but thrust him aside, and in their hearts they turned to Egypt, saying to Aaron, 'Make for us gods who will go before us. As for this Moses who led us out from the land of Egypt, we do not know what has become of him.'"
ACTS 7:39–40 ESV

Are you a bit stressed out? If so, look deep within. Check your heart. Is it yearning for the comfort of the enslavement you know? Has your heart turned to trusting in other gods—people, money, power, possessions? Have you rejected, thrust aside, the Lord of all, Jesus, who can help you rise above all things, who can free you from the bondage of stress?

Determine to embrace your new life as a free woman with the Maker of manna rather than go back to your old life as a slave, eating the garlic and onions of Egypt.

*I'm turning my heart—as well as my mind,
body, spirit, and soul—back to You, Lord.
You have freed me to live again—forever!*

Lady-in-Waiting

I look to you, heaven-dwelling God, look up to you for help.
Like servants, alert to their master's commands, like a
maiden attending her lady, we're watching and waiting,
holding our breath, awaiting your word of mercy.
PSALM 123:1–2 MSG

Sometimes it takes awhile to de-stress, like air slowly leaking out of a tire. And it may take even longer for our circumstances—or we ourselves—to change. But it will happen. The key is to change your attitude. Instead of being weighed down by what isn't right, buoy yourself by being grateful for what is right. Count those blessings. Then have patience, looking up to God, watching and waiting for Him to respond to your prayers for help. Most of all, be hope-filled and alert, knowing that His word will come and lift your heart.

So be grateful, patient, and hopeful. Before you know it, you'll hear God whisper in your ear, telling you the word you need to hear.

Lord, I'm Your lady-in-waiting, knowing
You will tell me just what I need to hear.

Mighty Things

Give us help for the hard task; human help is worthless. In God we'll do our very best; he'll flatten the opposition for good.
Psalm 60:11–12 msg

So many wonderful verses in the Bible give us hope and strength and help combat stress. God tells Isaiah, "Say to those who have an anxious heart, 'Be strong; fear not! Behold, your God . . . will come and save you' " (35:4 esv). And Psalm 60 tells us, "With God's help we will do mighty things" (verse 12 nlt). The proof of such words is revealed in the lives and stories of the heroes of our faith. Consider Stephen's declaration about God's follower Joseph: "God was with him and rescued him out of all his afflictions and gave him favor and wisdom before Pharaoh, king of Egypt, who made him ruler over Egypt" (Acts 7:9–10 esv).

The point is you need not give in to stress. Don't be afraid. Hand yourself and your circumstances over to God, knowing He'll save you, strengthen you, and help you do mighty things!

God, in You I can do mighty things!

Your Best Friend

*"Now you are my friends, since I have
told you everything the Father told me."*
JOHN 15:15 NLT

If you're in a period of waiting, you need not stress. You are
not alone. Jesus is right there with you.

Jesus is your friend. He has promised never to leave you or
forsake you. During this time of waiting, Jesus is helping you to
grow, to discover, to learn, to prepare for the next step in your
life. And in the process, He is keeping you calm by leading you
to the words you need to read and hear, the promises you need
to embrace, to give you the strength to become the person you
were created to be. He asks you to "be sure of this: I am with
you always" (Matthew 28:20 NLT). Because that's what a good,
strong, and wise friend does. He sticks close to His little sister,
the burgeoning princess who is the apple of His eye.

*Thanks for waiting it out with me, Jesus, my Brother,
Savior, and Friend. Teach and tell me more!*

A Well-Watered Tree

"Blessed are those who trust in the LORD and have made the LORD their hope and confidence. They are like trees planted along a riverbank, with roots that reach deep into the water. Such trees are not bothered by the heat or worried by long months of drought."
JEREMIAH 17:7–8 NLT

God says that "those who put their trust in mere humans, who rely on human strength. . . are like stunted shrubs in the desert, with no hope for the future. They will live in the barren wilderness" (verses 5–6 NLT). But those who trust in Him, whose hope and confidence are in Him, are like trees by the water. Not only are they undisturbed by what happens in their environment, but "their leaves stay green, and they never stop producing fruit" (verse 8 NLT).

You may not have the power to choose what happens to you, but you do have the power to change your attitude toward it. So trust in God, placing your hope and confidence in Him alone.

I'm making You my one and only hope, Lord.

Free and Endless Refills

Ever be filled and stimulated with the [Holy] Spirit.
EPHESIANS 5:18 AMPC

In this world you can turn to many different things to fulfill yourself, to satisfy your cravings for energy, strength, even peace. But turning to the world's salve can lead to even more stress. God would have you turn to Him. Remember, being filled with Him and His Spirit is not a once-and-done thing, happening only when you profess your belief in Jesus. It's a continual refilling.

So turn to God. Recognize that "you are God's temple and that God's Spirit dwells in you" (1 Corinthians 3:16 ESV). Daily pray for God to refresh you deep within, taking into account that just as you likely "know how to give good gifts [gifts that are to their advantage] to your children, how much more will your heavenly Father give the Holy Spirit to those who ask and continue to ask Him!" (Luke 11:13 AMPC).

Lord, I am looking to be filled by You and Your Spirit.
Refresh me now—over and over again!

True Reality

"GOD is with you, O mighty warrior!"
JUDGES 6:12 MSG

Gideon was trying to make the best of a stressful situation. The Midianites kept sending raiding parties into his territory. So Gideon was threshing wheat in his hiding place when an angel of God opened his eyes, calling him a "mighty warrior"! Gideon didn't feel that God was with him, nor that he, the least of his family, was anything but weak. But God again told him not to worry. That with God, Gideon was to "go with the strength you have, and rescue Israel from the Midianites" (Judges 6:14 NLT). Later, as Gideon did what God called him to do, "the Spirit of the LORD clothed Gideon with power" (Judges 6:34 NLT)—just when he needed it most.

Don't let your current situation stress you out. Know that God is with you and that you can move forward in the strength you have—because God will add His to it, just when you need it most.

*Help me to see the true reality I have with You in my life, Lord.
Help me to be Your mighty warrior!*

Come Away

The apostles returned to Jesus and told him all that they had done and taught. And he said to them, "Come away by yourselves to a desolate place and rest a while." For many were coming and going, and they had no leisure even to eat. And they went away in the boat to a desolate place by themselves.
MARK 6:30–32 ESV

A bit stressed? Feel as if you don't even have time to eat? Jesus knows exactly what you need.

First, go to Him and tell Him everything you have done. Then follow the same advice He gave His other workers. Come away. . .by yourself. . .to a quiet place. . .and rest awhile. It doesn't have to be far away, just far enough to get away from your "crowds." And you're to do it by yourself. Make sure the place you're heading to is away from people, distractions, and noise. Then, once you are there, take a deep breath. And "rest a while," moving from de-stressed to blessed.

I'm coming to meet with You, Lord.
I'm ready to rest in You.

Lying Back

Unless the LORD builds a house, the work of the builders is wasted. . . . It is useless for you to work so hard from early morning until late at night, anxiously working for food to eat; for God gives rest to his loved ones.
PSALM 127:1–2 NLT

Yes, God wants you to work on the house that's being built. But He doesn't want you to be laboring from 4:00 a.m. to midnight (unless perhaps you're laboring to bring a new life into this world). He wants you to put some trust in Him, that He will use for good whatever you are putting your hand to.

So trust that God has a good purpose and outcome for all the work you are doing. Trust that He will always provide for you. Then get some rest, lying back in His arms, falling asleep with His breath warming your ear.

I'm ready to change up my schedule, Lord, to get more of the rest I so sorely need and You so readily give.

Believe and Receive

Jesus met a man with an advanced case of leprosy. . . . "Lord,"
he said, "if you are willing, you can heal me and make me
clean." Jesus reached out and touched him. "I am willing," he
said. "Be healed!" And instantly the leprosy disappeared.
LUKE 5:12–13 NLT

God is willing to step into your situation and help you. He's
willing to reach out His hand and touch you, commanding
the problem to be solved, declaring you to be healed. Of this
you must be certain. But to be touched by the loving hand of
Jesus, you must meet up with Him. You must be as humble
in His presence as was this leper who "bowed with his face to
the ground" (verse 12 NLT). You must not doubt but know that
Jesus is willing, out of His love and compassion for you, to enter
into your situation and sort out your problem. Jesus is willing
to give—if you are willing to believe and receive.

Lord, shore up my faith. Help me to
be willing to believe and receive!

Protective Wall of Fire

The other angel said, "Hurry, and say to that young man,
'Jerusalem will someday be so full. . .there won't be room
enough for everyone! Many will live outside the city walls.
Then I, myself, will be a protective wall of fire around Jerusalem,
says the Lord. And I will be the glory inside the city!'"
ZECHARIAH 2:4–5 NLT

Imagine, God being a protective wall of fire around you—and the glory within you! Regarding verse 5, John Gill's *Exposition of the Entire Bible* says, "The Targum [an ancient Aramaic paraphrase or interpretation of the Hebrew Bible] paraphrases it, 'my Word shall be unto her, saith the Lord, as a wall of fire encompassing her round about.' "

When you feel stressed, remember God's protective wall of fire. Reach out with your heart and mind and pull in a word from God to keep the anxiety at bay, to feed the glory of His presence within you, to generate the calming warmth His Word alone can give.

Lord, I feel Your wall of fire protecting me!
May Your glory within keep stress without!

The Way to Turn

When I am overwhelmed, you alone know the way I should turn. . . . Then I pray to you, O Lord. I say, "You are my place of refuge. You are all I really want in life. . . . Bring me out of prison so I can thank you. . . for you are good to me."
PSALM 142:3, 5, 7 NLT

Even if stress causes us to lose direction, God will know the way we should go, the next steps we should take. But we need to reach out and tell Him where we are. It's not that He doesn't know. It's that we need to recognize (have an awareness of) the place we find ourselves in. Praying to Him will help us reaffirm our priorities and state the true reality of our situation.

In God, we have a place to run. He's all we need. In His power and strength, He'll "bring us out."

When I'm losing my way, You know my next steps. So I'm praying to You, Lord. Shower me with Your goodness!

Presence and Power

*The Lord brought us forth out of Egypt with a mighty hand
and with an outstretched arm, and with great (awesome)
power and with signs and with wonders.*

DEUTERONOMY 26:8 AMPC

Never doubt that God can get you out of a stressful situation.
He did it over and over again for His people—and will do it
over and over again for you. That is, of course, unless He wants
you to learn something while you're in your specific situation,
as He wanted the Israelites to trust in His promise to lead them
into the land of milk and honey instead of focusing on the false
reality of giants in that land. The point is to refrain from worry.
Don't stress or be anxious. Remain in His power and love. Know
that God is with you no matter what you're going through. And
that, when He's ready, He'll bring you out with a mighty hand
in an amazing way.

Thank You, Lord, for Your presence and power in my life.

Before, Behind, and Beside

You go before me and follow me.
You place your hand of blessing on my head.
PSALM 139:5 NLT

No matter what your worries are, you never face anything alone. God has gone before you and seen what's ahead. He'll be following behind you to protect you from the rear. And He's right here beside you, with His hand of blessing upon your head.

Keep these truths in the forefront of your mind and you'll see there's no reason to fret. God has everything under control—according to His plan, His timing, His ideas for you. So relax into all that's happening. Keep alert for the voice of the Spirit, telling you which way to go. Follow without fear, for you have the strongest being in the world—the God of the universe—before, behind, and beside you. You are blessed.

Lord, help me to constantly keep the reality of Your presence with me in my heart, mind, body, soul, and spirit. For I know with You a breath away, I have nothing to fear.

Everlasting Light

If I ride the wings of the morning, if I dwell by the farthest oceans, even there your hand will guide me, and your strength will support me. . . . How precious are your thoughts about me, O God. They cannot be numbered! . . . And when I wake up, you are still with me!
PSALM 139:9–10, 17–18 NLT

No matter how deep you get sucked under, no matter how long you stay in the stress zone, God will find you, pull you back out, guide you with His wisdom, and support you with His strength. You are on His mind, under His watchful eye night and day.

You may never be as dedicated to Him as He is to you. But you can take steps to get closer to Him by spending time in His presence and digging into His Word. Then ask Him to search your heart, to know your "anxious thoughts," to "point out anything" in you that offends Him, and to lead you "along the path of everlasting life" (verses 23–24 NLT).

You know all about me, Lord.
Help me to know Your path for me.

Bold as a Lion

*"Fear not, stand firm, and see the salvation of the Lord,
which he will work for you today. For the Egyptians
whom you see today, you shall never see again. The Lord
will fight for you, and you have only to be silent."*
Exodus 14:13–14 ESV

The Israelites had the Red Sea in front of them and Pharaoh's army behind them. It looked like there was no way out. But God had a plan. He told Moses, "Lift up your staff, and stretch out your hand over the sea and divide it, that the people of Israel may go through the sea on dry ground" (verse 16 ESV).

With walls of water on both sides of them, that's just what the Israelites did. "Bold as lions" (Proverbs 28:1 NLT), they walked through the seabed and gained the other side before the Egyptians could touch one stitch of their clothing.

Never feel trapped. Be bold as a lion. And watch the Lord fight for you!

*With You in my life, Lord, I need not fear.
Help me to stand firm in You.*

Labels

Jabez was a better man than his brothers, a man of honor. . . .
Jabez prayed to the God of Israel: "Bless me, O bless me!
Give me land, large tracts of land. And provide your personal
protection—don't let evil hurt me." God gave him what he asked.
1 CHRONICLES 4:9–10 MSG

Each one of us bears a label, whether it's given to us by our parents, peers, siblings, friends, or even ourselves. Our label might be skinny, chunky, weakling, cheat, addict, money-grabber, shark, poor, failure, etc. But life is stressful enough without wearing a badge of dishonor.

Jabez had a label. Having had a difficult labor, his mom named him "pain." But Jabez refused to see himself that way, to go through life with that misnomer. So he prayed with all his heart to God, asking Him to bless his life, give him more responsibility, and protect him. God granted his request.

What label do you need to leave at God's feet?

Lord, remove this label. Help me to see myself with
Your eyes—blessed, responsible, and protected.

How to Prevail

They were given help against them, and the Hagrites or Ishmaelites were delivered into their hands, and all who were allied with them, for they cried to God in the battle; and He granted their entreaty, because they relied on, clung to, and trusted in Him.

1 Chronicles 5:20 AMPC

Descendants of Reuben, Gad, and Manasseh, men described as "valiant" and "skillful in war" (verse 18 AMPC), went to war against the Hagrites and their allies. But during the battle, things must not have been going so well because the Israelites "cried to God." And He helped them prevail! Why? Because they "relied on, clung to, and trusted in" their God.

What battle are you waging? Have you cried out to God for help, or are you stressed out because you're trying to win the day in your own strength? Rely on God, cling to Him, know He is your Savior. And He will help you prevail.

I'm crying to You, Lord, trusting in You with all I am!

Breaking the Silence

The LORD detests the sacrifice of the wicked,
but he delights in the prayers of the upright.
PROVERBS 15:8 NLT

Sometimes we get so immersed in the happenings of this physical life that we forget to look up, to catch our breath, to spend time with the One who can lift us above all the stress and uncertainty that's weighing us down. We forget we have a God who loves to spend time with us. A God who delights in our prayers. A God who's leaning down, bending His ear to our lips, yearning for us to utter one little sound. He wants to help, guide, forgive, hold, carry, provide for, and love.

Know that God finds joy in your presence and is eager to listen to anything you have to say. So rant, rave, love, crave, plead, beg, or just babble about your day. But go to the One who longs to hear your voice. Break the silence. Pray.

Lord, thank You for being such a
wonderful God and friend. Let's talk.

Expectations

Love GOD, all you saints; GOD takes care of all
who stay close to him. . . . Be brave. Be strong.
Don't give up. Expect GOD to get here soon.
PSALM 31:23–24 MSG

It's important to evaluate your expectations. Are you hoping other people will give you some sort of break? That money will fall from the sky? That circumstances you can't control will miraculously change in your favor? Or are you sticking close to God, hoping in Him, expecting Him to take charge not just of your situation, but of you—mind, body, spirit, and soul?

No matter what's happening in your life, keep praying. Be like the psalmist who tells God: "Desperate, I throw myself on you: you are my God! Hour by hour I place my days in your hand" (verses 14–15 MSG). Then stay brave and strong, waiting for, hoping for, and expecting God to step into your midst any moment.

I'm never giving up, Lord. I'm sticking with You,
knowing You'll get me through.

Relax

How do you know what your life will be like tomorrow?
Your life is like the morning fog—it's here a little while,
then it's gone. What you ought to say is, "If the Lord
wants us to, we will live and do this or that."
JAMES 4:14–15 NLT

We're women. Upon awakening, we usually have a mental plan for what we'll wear, what work needs to get done, what meals we're going to cook, what pick-ups and drop-offs are required, and what pleasures we may be able to partake in before bed. But then something happens. We get interrupted by an unplanned event, circumstance, or obligation. And yet we still try to work out our day according to our schedule, holding on to our original plan with a white-knuckled grip, causing stress within and without.

No more! Relax. Allow some things to fall by the wayside. Take the attitude that "if the Lord wants us to, we will live and do this or that." And let the chips fall where they may.

My day is in Your hands, Lord. Now I can relax!

His Once Again

*The Lord your God is in your midst. . .he will rejoice
over you with gladness; he will quiet you by his love;
he will exult over you with loud singing.*

ZEPHANIAH 3:17 ESV

Feeling alone? As if the world is on your shoulders, weighing
you down? As if you can't take one more day of this stress?
Step back and give a shrug, allowing the world to roll off your
shoulders. Then look right in front of you. There is God. He is
right there with you, living, working, playing by your side. He
is grinning from ear to ear, so glad He is that you are with Him.
He's going to soothe you with His great love, going to rid you
of all the things you fear. And once that balm is applied, once
the stress is no longer clouding your vision and stopping up
your ears, He's going to celebrate by singing over you.

Step back. Look straight ahead. "God is in your midst."
Listen to His song!

*Sing to me, Lord. Love me; ease my mind and heart.
Make me Yours once again.*

Mighty Wind

When the enemy shall come in like a flood, the Spirit of the Lord will. . .put him to flight [for He will come like a rushing stream which the breath of the Lord drives].

ISAIAH 59:19 AMPC

No matter how much stress tries to drown you, a greater force is ready to come in "like a rushing stream." A force no power can withstand: the Spirit of the Lord. He's a mighty wind, ready to blow you out of whatever dark waters you may be in.

Your only job is to walk close to Him; to obey His command to love Him with all you are and love others as yourself; and, of course, to pray. You can't have any kind of relationship with anyone—either your Father in heaven or others on earth—unless you have open lines of communication, lines through which you speak and listen.

Know God is here for you. Trust Him to blow any negatives, bad attitudes, and stressors out of your waters. Pray for His breath to deliver you now.

Lord, put my negative thoughts to flight.
Then flood me with Your never-ending love.

Truth

Jesus said, "I am the Road, also the Truth, also the Life.
No one gets to the Father apart from me. If you really
knew me, you would know my Father as well. From
now on, you do know him. You've even seen him!"
JOHN 14:6–7 MSG

In this world of "fake news" where we are surrounded by loads of misinformation, it's wonderfully reassuring to delve into the truth of God's Word written thousands of years ago, wisdom that has stood the test of time. How comforting and amazing that we have access to and can follow the Word that reveals God the Father to us, helping us to know Him and what He would have us do.

Keep the truth, wisdom, and knowledge the Bible provides close to your heart. Write it on the walls of your mind. Cling to it amid trials and you'll find a peace that surpasses all understanding. Stay on the Road, stick to the Truth, and you'll be living the Life God has planned for you and those you love.

You, Lord, are my Truth.

God Alone

*For God alone, O my soul, wait in silence, for my hope is
from him. He only is my rock and my salvation, my fortress;
I shall not be shaken. . . . Trust in him at all times. . .pour
out your heart before him; God is a refuge for us.*
PSALM 62:5–6, 8 ESV

When stress comes knocking at your door, remember to breathe.
Then calm your heart by reminding your soul to wait in silence.
Know that your hope is in God alone. He's the firm foundation
you can stand tall on, the solid Rock, the Unchanging One. He's
the One who saves you—over and over again. He's the One you
can run to, the One who is always there for you.

Because God is in your life, nothing can shake you up. So
breathe. Then pour out your heart to the One you trust. The
One who protects you, who is your ultimate shelter in the storm
and in the sun. He's waiting.

*Here's my heart, Lord. I come to You for peace,
for assurance, for help, for sanctuary, for love.*

God's Goodness

No doubt about it! God is good—good to good people,
good to the good-hearted. But I nearly missed it, missed
seeing his goodness. I was looking the other way.
PSALM 73:1–3 MSG

Sometimes, when our eyes drift away from God, we find them settling onto people who seem to have made it further than we have. Ones who, although they are less than godly, seem to be blessed. We then wonder what we have to do, how much harder we have to work, to have the "good life." And we become stressed out trying to make it in this world.

This is when we need to turn our eyes to Jesus, realizing that those who are living without Him will "never be heard from again" (verse 27 MSG). Nevertheless, we may say, "But I'm in the very presence of GOD—oh, how refreshing it is! I've made Lord GOD my home" (verse 28 MSG).

I know it's good for me to be near You, Lord.
You are my refuge, my life, my heart, my all.

Brimming Over

Oh! May the God of green hope fill you up with joy, fill you up with peace, so that your believing lives, filled with the life-giving energy of the Holy Spirit, will brim over with hope!
ROMANS 15:13 MSG

Having hope can be a major de-stressor. It's about putting your worries aside and focusing on what could be. That doesn't mean you take a dreamy stance, just wondering what will happen next while you wait on the sidelines. It involves your taking some kind of action, giving all you can, doing all you can, to make that hope a reality. Yet at the same time, you're to put the entire situation, person, problem, or issue into God's hands. For in Him is your true hope. No matter what happens, you trust in the One who has your best interests at heart, the One who knows all, who sees beyond what you see, who will do what is best for His world, His people, His planet.

My hope is in You, Lord! I'm brimming over!

Lift

The Lord is my Strength and my [impenetrable] Shield;
my heart trusts in, relies on, and confidently leans on Him,
and I am helped; therefore my heart greatly rejoices, and
with my song will I praise Him. . . . Save Your people. . .
nourish and shepherd them and carry them forever.

PSALM 28:7, 9 AMPC

When we have nothing left within us—no energy, no strength, no light—we must reach out, cry out to the One who has all the answers, who can hold us safely in His arms until we are able to rise again and carry on—for Him.

So lift your arms toward heaven. Call on your Rock, Refuge, and Fortress. Allow His power to flow into you as you rest quietly, calmly in His arms. Trust Him to handle all you cannot, to work out those situations in which you see no way out. Allow Him to be your strength. Then sing your song of praise as He brings you back into the light.

I lift my eyes and arms to You, Lord.

Precious

"When you pass through the waters, I will be with you; and through the rivers, they shall not overwhelm you; when you walk through fire you shall not be burned, and the flame shall not consume you. For I am the LORD your God. . . . You are precious in my eyes. . . . Fear not, for I am with you."
ISAIAH 43:2–5 ESV

When you're stressed, you feel as if you're walking alone. As if no one knows what you're really going through or sees how much you're suffering. You feel as if you're drowning in a flood and no one hears your cries. Having been burned so many times, you feel as if you're walking through fire. You wonder who, if anyone, can save you.

Then you hear a voice, feel a touch, sense a presence. You taste something good. It's the Holy Spirit reaching out for you, walking right beside you, strong and mighty to save. God is with you, and you are precious in His eyes. Impress this truth upon your mind.

I will not fear, Lord, for You are beside me.

A New Way

Thus says the Lord, Who makes a way through the sea and a path through the mighty waters. . . . Do not [earnestly] remember the former things; neither consider the things of old. Behold, I am doing a new thing! Now it springs forth; do you not perceive and know it and will you not give heed to it? I will even make a way in the wilderness and rivers in the desert.

ISAIAH 43:16, 18–19 AMPC

You have chosen to walk a new road. To trust the One who makes a way where you can see no way, the One who has forgiven and forgotten all the mistakes you've made.

So put your hand in the hand of the One who is ready to do a new thing in your life. Forget what has passed. Look to God in confidence, knowing He has already cleared a path for you, the precious daughter He has called by name (see Isaiah 43:1). Answer His call and walk forward in His presence.

Lord, thank You for being my peace and my life.

Scripture Index